The Intimate Edges of Psychotherapy for Complex Trauma

The Intimate Edges of Psychotherapy for Complex Trauma is a personal account of an analysis spanning more than 20 years, written by practicing psychoanalysts.

This book is the first to document an on-going analysis where both analyst and analysand are seasoned psychologists capable of articulating the relational analytic process theoretically and personally. Rebecca Klott shares a narrative of complex, severe sexual and emotional trauma, with commentary provided by her analyst, Richard Raubolt. Klott and Raubolt create an embodied dialogue, exposing what treatment is like for both the severely traumatized patient and the clinician tasked with helping the patient work toward healing. Through this intimate vantage point, the reader journeys with both patient and clinician as they encounter the breakdowns and breakthroughs that are a part of the process of healing.

The Intimate Edges of Psychotherapy for Complex Trauma will be essential reading for clinicians, trainees, and students in the fields of psychoanalysis, psychoanalytic psychotherapy, counseling, social work, and counseling and clinical psychology.

Rebecca Klott, PhD, is a licensed counseling psychologist. She is the founder and president of River City Psychological Services, a group practice in Grand Rapids, Michigan. She also writes psychologically focused fictional works.

Richard Raubolt is a licensed clinical psychologist and board-certified psychoanalyst. He has written three books, published over 30 professional papers, and produced five films on the intersection of applied psychoanalysis and social-cultural issues. In over 45 years of practice, Richard has presented his work nationally and internationally.

Loray Daws is a registered clinical psychologist in South Africa and British Columbia, Canada. He is currently in private practice and serves as a senior faculty member at the International Masterson Institute and as a board member and teaching faculty at the Object Relations Institute in New York. Loray specializes in psychoanalysis and Dasein analysis and is the author and editor of eight books on psychoanalysis and existential analysis.

"A psychoanalytic memoir of unimaginable impacts and survival. At the heart of such catastrophe, Faith lies dormant, awaiting rebirth of psyche and soul. Damaged and damaging bonds finally housed, finding psyche-soul deformations transformed, the shattered and shattering impacts of childhood trauma infused with life-giving capacity. As written by Lord Byron and articulated by Daws – Here's to the Children of the Second Birth."

Dr. Michael Eigen, psychoanalyst and author of
Bits of Psyche: Selected Seminars by Michael Eigen

"This courageously intimate and unflinchingly honest page-turner, co-created by Dr. Richard Raubolt (analyst) and Dr. Rebecca Klott (analysand), offers readers an extraordinary glimpse into the profound heartbreak of severe, complex childhood trauma, the messiness of human suffering, and the intricacies of the healing process. Sustained by Raubolt's faith in the transformative power of a co-created 'we,' Rebecca, even in her darkest moments, finds solace in the knowledge that she is no longer alone. The rawness of Rebecca's heartrending experiences and the incisiveness of Raubolt's penetrating insights are woven together with such tenderness and love that this becomes a story not just about therapy but about the shared humanity of two brave souls journeying in tandem from lost to found."

Martha Stark, MD, award-winning author of nine
books on the integration of psychoanalytic theory with
clinical practice, including *Modes of Therapeutic Action*,
Working with Resistance, and *Relentless Hope*

"This memoir pushes the boundaries of modern psychoanalytic treatment in a way that deepens what Freud coined as 'the talking cure.' In these pages one finds a combination of talking and writing that blends emotional depths with theoretical moorings, while a beautiful, painful story unfolds."

Keri S. Cohen, co-editor of *Toxic Nourishment and
Damaged Bonds in the Work of Michael Eigen:
Working with the Obstructive Object*

The Intimate Edges of Psychotherapy for Complex Trauma

In Tandem

Rebecca Klott, Richard Raubolt, and Loray Daws

Foreword by Rachel Newcombe

Routledge
Taylor & Francis Group
LONDON AND NEW YORK

Designed cover image: Getty | Yana Iskayeva

First published 2025
by Routledge
4 Park Square, Milton Park, Abingdon, Oxon OX14 4RN

and by Routledge
605 Third Avenue, New York, NY 10158

Routledge is an imprint of the Taylor & Francis Group, an informa business

British Library Cataloguing-in-Publication Data
A catalogue record for this book is available from the British Library

ISBN: 978-1-032-99539-7 (hbk)
ISBN: 978-1-032-99538-0 (pbk)
ISBN: 978-1-003-60472-3 (ebk)

DOI: 10.4324/9781003604723

Typeset in Times New Roman
by Apex CoVantage, LLC

Contents

Foreword

Rebecca and Raubolt: The Creation of a We-Ness

> I believe every good clinician should have a working knowledge of how attachment, when wounded, leaves deep scars that impact every relationship . . .
>
> Rebecca

> . . . exploration, imagination and reverie – the stuff of therapy.
>
> Raubolt

I imagine there will be readers of this book who want to analyze and/or judge a clinical tale co-authored by a patient and an analyst. In this story, the patient is also a therapist.

However tempted you are to judge this dyad writing together, please don't. I am asking, requesting, that you suspend judgment, quell your anxieties, and allow yourself to listen to what is being said between Rebecca, the patient, and Raubolt, the analyst.

> The most painful and important area where I'm growing is in believing that I matter to others, that I don't disappear for them when I'm not present. This fear impacts so many parts of my life, but most painfully, it creates the sense of aloneness that overwhelms me.
>
> Rebecca

> Rebecca, and so our work together continues but now with greater subtlety and nuance. We talk more about the leading edge, which is where you are going, and less about where you have been.
>
> Raubolt

It has taken me time to write this foreword because I want to make sure that I introduce this embodied work with respect and care.

You see, I, too, am an analyst, and like Rebecca, I, too, have been and am a patient. My hunch is that many people reading this right now have also been both patient and analyst, which is why I want you to take a pause now. Think about your own therapy and the personal uniqueness of your relationship with your therapist. If you can imagine someone reading about your relationship, what are you most concerned about? And what would you want your readers to understand about your relationship with your therapist? Lastly, what do you imagine if your reader critiqued this very personal work instead of accepting it as an offering, as a vehicle to show the nature of therapy?

Rebecca shares her motivations when she addresses us directly in the opening of the book when she begins *Dear Colleagues*. She asks, "I, myself, wondered what I hoped to accomplish by writing this book. I've wondered what it was that I believed I needed to say." From the start, she lets us in on her writing process,

> I sometimes retell about a trauma much later in the text. In the second or third telling, I often will describe the incident with more detail or offer a different perspective on what happened. While this was not done intentionally, it does simulate how psychotherapy often works.

One of the many highlights of this book is that it reads like a lyrical narrative timeline, and how we tell our life stories in therapy. There is never a beginning, middle, or end.

Unlike a novel that has a traditional story arch, this book is a fluid conversation, navigating the telling of traumatic events and how they emerge in the present with Raubolt.

> In our exchanges throughout the book, you will witness how each of us, individually, move toward a "we." It is this "we" in any successful psychotherapy relationship that is the force that heals. It is the force, separate from the analyst and the patient, but created by the combination of their joined effort aimed at guiding the patient through the mud and grime of trauma.

This is what the reader will experience as the "We-ness" that is co-created between Rebecca and Raubolt, the idiosyncratic beauty that occurs when two people share a mission of entering into the unknown.

In his book *Terrors and Experts* (1997), Adam Phillips asks, "What must be given up in order to speak?"

Rebecca and Raubolt allow us to see an answer to this question by showing us their interactions. Often, we fear what will happen when we speak about the most traumatic events of our lives, and only after having done so are we able to experience what speaking does. In one of his responses to Rebecca, Raubolt says,

> Rebecca, those who would dismiss psychoanalytic therapy as merely a talking therapy underestimate the power of language.

Because Rebecca and Raubolt have shared themselves with us, I'd like to share with you a dream I had the evening before I would meet with Rebecca, Raubolt (the only person who I know), and Loray, the person writing the last chapter of this book.

* * * * *

I am sitting at my dining room and a female comes in and sits at the head and Raubolt comes in and sits at the other head. We are all reading something. I am concerned that the woman and I might not be on the same page, yet I know it will be okay. Then Raubolt, who is at the other end of the table, gets up and goes into my living room, on a table where I do Zoom meetings is a beautiful bird cage. Raubolt goes over to the cage and opens the door and a small bird flies out and perches on the arm of my couch. Richard is quietly talking to the bird and the bird seems to know what he is saying; they are in conversation. I know we are waiting for another man to join us.

* * * * *

I shared this dream with Rebecca, Raubolt, and Loray Daws because I felt it was a prophetic dream, an unconscious communication, and a we-ness as a result of reading the book.

Most astonishing, or not given the nature of our work, is that after I shared the dream, Rebecca moved her chair to the side and showed me a bird cage she had in her office.

Throughout this book, you will have an opportunity to travel with Rebecca as she speaks of her traumas and evolving trust in her analyst, Raubolt, sojourners of the human condition.

In the spirit of sharing like Rebecca and Raubolt have done, I want to share something my analyst said to me recently. "Maybe our work is about two people finding a way to reach each other." This is certainly what Rebecca and Raubolt have done, and they include us in their reaching.

Rebecca, a profoundly wise therapist and writer, addresses Raubolt, a profoundly wise analyst and writer, and says,

So, Raubolt, here we are some 20 years later. Through the "we" of our therapy relationship, I have been able to reclaim so many parts of myself which were terribly wounded by severe, complex childhood trauma that reverberated into my adulthood. It took both of us and the co-created "we" to get me here.

Thank you, Rebecca and Raubolt, for the gift of including us in your We-ness. I am certain that this book will speak to every reader.

Rachel Newcombe

Reference

Phillips, A. (1997). *Terrors and Experts*. Harvard University Press.

Letter to the Reader

Dear Colleagues,

You may have picked this book up uncertain of what you would find. Would this be a tell-all memoir of unspeakable abuse? Perhaps, instead, you expected a psychotherapy textbook, a cool and clinical explanation regarding the fall-out that occurs as a result of complex, multigenerational abuse and trauma. Or, potentially, it would be a treatise on the newest theory or therapeutic model for this difficult-to-treat population. Some whiz-bang fix that could bring peace in fewer than 12 sessions.

I, myself, wondered what I hoped to accomplish by writing this book. I've wondered what it was that I believed I needed to say. What my mind, in fact, demanded I tell about my journey through extreme sexual and emotional abuse. I've not been compelled because the abuse was so horrific, though it was. Instead, I've felt a responsibility to explore how I was able to cobble together a life of relationships with others and, more importantly, a relationship with myself despite these traumas.

In truth, my plan, at times, felt vague. I knew that I did not want to write a detailed account in which I chronicled memory after memory of abuse by my family. I did need, however, to share "broad strokes" regarding what happened. I knew I needed to record what is necessary in order to convey my message to you. But, I also shared memories of my own psychotherapy. I share the moments when I was helped, when I was healed.

This psychotherapy memoir is written in tandem with my psychoanalyst, Dr. Richard Raubolt. Together, we weave our own understandings about how we were able to create a space for my wounded parts to find respite and where I could grow beyond the traumatic events that had shaped me. Writing together, we described how we created a framework of witnessing the trauma. You will notice that in the text, I am writing directly to Dr. Raubolt. I do this for a couple of reasons. It helped me feel safe enough to write about some of the most difficult moments of my life if I envisioned it as part of a conversation I was having with him. It also allowed for a level of intimacy for you, readers. We wanted you to have the chance to watch as the story of my trauma and healing unfolded in as raw and unfiltered form as possible. In this manner of telling, you will not hear an edited and editorialized, cleaned-up explanation of the treatment of trauma.

At times, I shared bits of memories, though I tried to avoid graphic details, both for my own well-being and for yours. I've already talked through many of the details of my trauma and did not see any need to cleave myself open outside of the therapy room. And, as clinicians, you have already, or, if you're a newer clinician, will soon hear tales of trauma that will haunt you. I do not wish for you to be visited by my ghosts.

You may notice that, at times, I will describe part of a trauma, suddenly change topics, and then later return to the original trauma story. I sometimes retell about a trauma much later in the text. In the second or third telling, I often will describe the incident with more detail or offer a different perspective on what happened. While this was not done intentionally, it does simulate how psychotherapy often works. Patients often will tell about the same experience multiple times, each retelling from a different place or perspective.

At other times, I focused on my relationship with Dr. Raubolt from my perspective. I hoped to speak both to the uniqueness of our relationship and the universality of the therapeutic relationship. I attempted to speak to the ingredients I believe are necessary in the patient-clinician dyad when the patient experiences the level of trauma that "forms and deforms the personality," as Judith Herman wrote (1997). I will share some of the moments when I felt, at a visceral level, that I was not a lone "survivor" but instead knew I was accompanied on a road emerging from darkness.

You will find Dr. Raubolt's responses within the text (written in a different font for identification purposes). He will both offer witness to his experiences as my clinician and his knowledge of and experiences with trauma in general. In our exchanges throughout the book, you will witness how each of us, individually, move toward a "we."

It is this "we" in any successful psychotherapy relationship that is the force that heals. It is the force, separate from the analyst and the patient, but created by the combination of their joint effort aimed at guiding the patient through the mud and grime of trauma. Dr. Raubolt is not, himself, healing me, a passive person waiting to be healed. And, I am not doing all of this alone while he sits in witness. It is "we" who journey toward a new growth. We offer a look at each of our perspectives of the various stages of our therapy relationship to the present day.

I also shared my observations as a "wounded healer." Having been a clinician for more than 25 years and a patient for longer, I have wandered on the road through the darkness created by complex trauma with others. I have walked beside them as they made their way toward healing. I will share some of the struggles and joys I've experienced as a person with her own significant trauma as I bear witness to the experiences of their trauma and their own journeys through it.

The underlying hope we have for this book is to help clinicians, particularly young practitioners, understand trauma from the inside out. Most books written about the topic of complex trauma have been written from the outside in. There is a "telling about" without a genuine understanding of what it means to experience and live with complex trauma. Theory and treatment, particularly those aimed at being "evidence based," have been largely developed and researched by academics. For those of us who have been the recipients of these treatments, there can be a sense that we remain unseen at best. At worst, we can feel like we are beyond repair when the "evidence based treatment" does not work.

As Dr. Raubolt and I worked on this project, we knew we wanted to invite you, the reader, into our clinical hours. So, in this spirit, we now ask you to join us in viewing, unvarnished and raw, what treatment is like for both the severely traumatized patient and the clinician tasked with helping the patient work toward healing. From this perspective, we believe you will get a more intimate, and thus deeper, sense of what it means and what is required to do this type of work. If you are not a survivor of complex trauma, this approach could allow you to grasp the patient's healing experience more viscerally than is often possible when only hearing from the clinician's point of view. If you have sustained complex trauma, our hope is that you will see, through reading about my journey, that you are not alone nor beyond help and that there are clinicians willing and able to journey with you. As Dr. Raubolt aptly reflected, "There are plenty of theoretical texts, explanations of treatment issues, and even relational analysis of patients. What is lacking is the discussion of the therapy process from both sides of the couch." We wrote this book to help fill some of that void.

As you read this book, we hope that you will witness the possibility of healing profound trauma. In a field that sometimes portrays a kind of hopelessness disguised in clinical labels, we tell the story of how together (patient and analyst) can create a relational foundation from which healing could take hold. In the telling of this story, we hope you will notice the characteristics we each bring to this healing relationship and that your observations will lead to a deepening of your understanding of trauma and the psychotherapy that can mend those damaged by it.

Chapter 1

The Beginning

Hello Raubolt,

I'm addressing you as "Raubolt" instead of "Richard" or "Dr. Raubolt" because when I'm speaking to you in my mind, I call you "Raubolt." If I'm going to use my own voice in this book, and not the voice of some professional, learned person, I should begin by talking to you using the name I have used for the two decades during which I've known you.

I have to admit that this narrative is a difficult thing to begin. How does one start to talk about some of the most intimate moments of one's life? There are so many roads in front of me. Which one to take first? I suppose we should begin at the beginning of my relationship with psychotherapy, in general. I think this might give some context for how I felt about myself and whether I was going to heal at all when our relationship began. What do you think?

Raubolt's Voice

Hello Rebecca, I tried out a few different formats in responding to you. For now, at least, I thought it best to respond from "within" your text, hoping this might give a more immediate feel to my writing. At any rate, I believe a review of your therapy experiences before we began helps inform how we worked together over the years. From the beginning, I was not and could never be a tabula rasa to you. There was too much history from previous psychotherapists who were there before me, replete with successes and failures but mostly with incompleteness (or that is as close as I can get to the feeling I had in meeting you).

I'd seen several therapists as a teenager and young adult. Most of them worked in some kind of agency – a community mental health center or a nonprofit agency of some kind. I met my first therapist at 16, and while I cannot remember her name and have no way of "measuring progress," I do know that I felt the woman wanted to help me and wanted me to feel safe. I knew, in my bones, that she believed

DOI: 10.4324/9781003604723-1

I could feel better than I did, and that was enough for me to continue to hope through those terrible years before adulthood.

Raubolt's Voice

Exactly. This felt safety, this profoundly moving experience of being believed in, especially when we can't feel it ourselves, is the lifeline that keeps us buoyant when we most fear drowning in grief.

Not all of those early clinicians were as invested in me, or, at least, it didn't feel like they were. I once had a therapist fall asleep in my session. Having now done the job of psychotherapy myself for over 25 years, I know that we clinicians are all human beings with flaws and limits. We have bad days. I know that we all have lives away from our patients that can impact how we are in the session. We go through losses, times of sadness, and boredoms. I know that while we are the only session for each of our clients, their sessions are sandwiched between several other sessions through which we travel.

I would like to say here, though, that I wish the therapist who had fallen asleep while I told him about feeling like I wanted to die had canceled his day or told me that he was sleepy and struggling to be awake, because I took from this experience that I wasn't important, and was, instead, probably someone so despicable that I wasn't worth being awake for. I was psychiatrically hospitalized two days after this session – a scarring and scary experience that changed me, wounded me deeply.

Raubolt's Voice

Rebecca, I remember you telling me this story. It was a simple thing you were asking for (paying for?) from this therapist and something that should have been offered without request – the decency of attention – listening to and being with you as you began to unfurl your story. Yes, we, as therapists, can grow distracted or preoccupied. It is, or should be, part of our job description to recognize when we are "off" and attend to this first so we can be with those we see in therapy. And, it is simply not done often enough. Sadly, it is often easier to blame the patient for a therapist's boredom.

Let us look more closely at this issue of therapist sleepiness you raise. Sleep can be an expression of a current experience which on the surface has little to do with the patient. It may be the result of ill health, lack of proper self-care, or fatigue rooted in anxiety or depression, for example. Yet, once it enters the treatment room, sleepiness becomes a clinical issue, reflecting the nature of the current relationship. For whatever the reason the therapist is falling asleep on the patient, a particular patient at a particular time, which, if not addressed, can have, as in your case, calamitous effects. I believe it is best examined initially as a resistance on the therapist's part to fully attach to the patient, and by failing to do so, the sleepiness keeps the therapist detached as well from the searing pain, terror, and helplessness so much a part of complex trauma. Such sleepiness may be initially experienced as boredom, which is easier to rationalize and lay at the patient's feet, but either way, it must not pass by unnoticed and undiscussed. If handled responsively, there is much to be gained in authentic relating and basic trust in the process which were so sorely lacking in the treatment you describe.

I would often start therapy and have to end pretty quickly because the agency where I was being seen had a limited allotment of sessions. Or, the therapist would leave for another position. Or, I could not afford to continue paying whatever amount I'd been asked to pay. I usually had to pay for my own therapy, even in high school, and if I didn't have a job at the time, I couldn't continue.

Sometimes, I would feel like I'd failed the clinicians I was seeing because I wouldn't get better. I would continue to have nightmares, flashbacks, a sense that everything was terrible. The low-grade sense of terror persisted despite using their breathing exercises, their worksheets about challenging thoughts, the endless workbooks about surviving sexual abuse. It wasn't that those things didn't help – they did. And, they didn't. They helped me have some framework for why I was so messed up – understanding that I wasn't the only person who'd been sexually abused helped. Knowing how to slow my breathing down helped, too, as did trying to think about things differently. Except when the terror was so high that nothing worked. When that happened, I just felt like I needed to die because I was not only damaged but a complete failure, because if I could just do what I was told would help . . . but, I couldn't.

Raubolt's Voice

Too true here. In a field overrun with techniques and methods, how does therapy proceed when these shiny, "wowing" therapies fail as they most always do? You point out the structure they can provide, or as temporary measures to relieve some of the most troubling symptoms when terror strikes. But it is always, in my estimation, the relationship that heals. The therapeutic relationship I am positing is characterized by responsiveness to the unique and individual needs of the patient, and, as such, includes steadfastness, authenticity, creativity, non-romantic love, curiosity, and respectful patience (waiting without expectations). I will say more about this topic later. Here, I want to begin articulating our framework as it evolved working together.

By the time I was at college, I'd begun to doubt psychotherapy would have any lasting impact. I would feel some relief when I was in treatment, some sense that I could make it through pain if only there was someone else who would know about the pain, but as soon as therapy ended, I would backslide quickly. I thought I might have to figure it all out on my own. Or, worse, I was destined to walk around with a searing pain that would never end.

Sometimes, remembering that pain takes my breath away. It used to sneak up on me, catching me unaware, and double me over. I would break into a cold sweat, feel as though I should open my veins and bleed out whatever toxin was causing so much pain, even if that would mean death. Because death would feel better than this. Still today, every now and then – maybe once a year – I will physically remember that pain, and I weep for that younger self who walked around the world, excelled at school, sang in my church choir, tried to make friends, or fall in love or just grow up, while carrying this pain.

I was psychiatrically hospitalized when I was 20 years old. That therapist I mentioned earlier had fallen asleep in our session, and I was desperate to find help. I spoke to a professor in my psychology program, asking for a referral. Something about my face must have tipped her off to how bad things were because she began to assess me for suicidal risk. I was so naive that I thought I could be honest about feeling suicidal but not having intent, and I ended up spending two weeks in a locked facility. It was terrifying – knowing I couldn't leave, couldn't stand outside as the sky released the first snow from its slate gray clouds, couldn't head to an all-night diner, couldn't use a phone whenever I wanted to call a friend. All because I'd said, "Yes, I think about suicide, and yes, I know how I would do it."

Raubolt's Voice

Rebecca, while it is admirable, to be honest, there are limits. What you counted on was kindness and attention with a bit of direction and hope. Instead, you received another's anxiety and panic. Why is it, I wonder, that we find it so hard to stand still and be with the pain of living?

No one acknowledged the second thing I'd said, "But I won't do it, because I know it would be wrong." At the end of my stay in that hospital, one of the art therapists said, "It's okay if you need to come back. People like you, with so much trauma, usually are in and out of hospitals throughout their lives."

The first time I met you, Raubolt, I was coming to see you with my then-boy-friend-later-husband, Jack. We were on the brink of ending our relationship, but we wanted to find a way to make it work. A work friend of ours had recommended you. He'd said that you were the best for therapists in the area, and Jack and I were both therapists. We'd met while working together at a nearby community mental health facility.

It became clear fairly quickly that couples counseling wasn't going to be successful – not because of you but because of a more complicated issue in Jack and my relationship that I don't want to get into. But, it became very clear to me that I wanted to see you for my own treatment. And, you agreed to see me. I don't really know how to explain the feeling I had sitting in your office during those couple's sessions other than to say that I could feel your genuine interest and care – something I didn't always feel when meeting with therapists, both personally and professionally.

I'm going to pivot here. I apologize for getting off topic, but I want to talk a little about our most recent session. It was painful for me, and I think for you, as well. I should preface that I'm slightly feverish as I'm writing today. COVID got me finally after three years of avoiding the damned virus. So, I might be a bit more emotional about things, but maybe that's okay. Because it was an emotional session, and I'd hoped to see you to process it earlier this week but could not because of the virus.

We were angry with each other in the session. I was angry about something you'd said in a previous session, something that reminded me that you see other patients. You admitted you were angry with me because you felt I was criticizing you. I felt like you were punishing me because you'd not responded to an email I'd sent to you. It felt like it was the closest I've ever felt to a standoff within our relationship because, for the first time in my memory, I knew you were angry with me. I felt like I wanted to back off, to apologize so that we could go back to liking each other. But I also didn't want to back off because I felt like I do that so often in order to keep people in my life, only to feel they're in my life because I let them treat me however they want to treat me.

I worried you were going to fire me from therapy. I also feared I might fire you because I felt so hurt. And, then, we somehow worked it out.

Raubolt's Voice

Yes, we worked something out. We always do. Even though feelings were running high for both of us, we have a long, dedicated history. The strength of this relationship is what allowed me the room to tell you I was angry with you even as I was absorbing your anger with me. I am not being cavalier or dismissive of the therapeutic crisis that developed. I am saying, as painful and disconcerting as it was, I did not think either of us would leave. Each of us is invested in an outcome that reflects the amount of change (growth) that has been achieved in our work together. And for the record, I learned some time ago that patients don't change unless their therapists do as well. In my clinical opinion, our relationship has, at its foundation, a true reciprocity, allowing for symmetricity within an asymmetrical relationship. The definition of true reciprocity I am using consists of: 1) There is intended mutual benefit to the patient and therapist, that is both grow emotionally and changes each. 2) There is a "nucleus of true attachment," to borrow a phrase developed by the Portuguese analyst Joao Pedro Diaz, who posits, "Two can be, think and feel as one (unconscious identification) although they remain two separate, differentiated 'co-workers' (conscious complementarity)" (Diaz, personal communication, June 15, 2024).

In that session, I expressed yet again how terrible it feels to love you so much and to know that I'm not as important to you as you are to me. I used the words "unrequited love" for the first time – it became so clear that it feels like just that – a love that goes unmet. And, I realized that it's how I felt throughout my childhood, that I loved and loved and loved, and at best, I was tolerated, occasionally acknowledged, but usually when something was taken from me. And, in that session, the weighty pain of it all crushed every bone inside of me. I wished I could sink down and die from that longing – to finally stop having to walk under the weight of it.

You said, "You're learning to love and trust at the same time."

The next day, I got on a plane to meet my friends for the once-delayed (COVID) birthday trip (which led to my current COVID condition). That sentence, "You're learning to love and trust at the same time," flew with me, sat in the seat next to me, grabbed hold of me, and choked me on that flight. Tears streamed down my face, soaking my mask. Maybe that's when I got COVID?

You have this strange gift of saying things that pierce to the very core of me and leave me uncertain of what I know about myself and the world. Were you trying to answer my eternal question of whether I matter to someone else?

Raubolt's Voice

I said those words to you as they seemed the best description I could offer. I was describing what I saw in the moment, knowing we would unpack the meaning(s) later. If I am in tune with you, I trust what I see, knowing that even if I am off the mark, therapy will move forward. Mistakes are not to be avoided when intentions are good. Additionally, as you know, I often choose to say less rather than more. Too many words accompany explanations or interpretations that are more confusing and distancing than insightful. Particularly when feelings are intense, I believe brief evocative reflections are the order of the day. For the record, I would also note I write in much the same manner.

Were you reminding me that this is all part of the process of attachment? God. How terrible and brutal and gorgeous in its destruction of the wall that separated us. And, you did it while you were angry with me.

This isn't to say I didn't have a right to be angry with you, or that you didn't have a right to be angry with me. I believe now, looking back, that it was several steps of missing each other, but I suppose that's what most arguments are about – misunderstanding the other. You were not your perfect self in that session, and neither was I.

Raubolt's Voice

And I want to write: Thank God.

But, I suppose I'm trying to say in the imperfectness of the session, you reached through and touched my pain, and I let you reach through and touch my pain. And, maybe, that's really what healing is about – both people imperfectly getting through pain.

Raubolt's Voice

Yes, yes, and yes.

Okay, there's my feverish commentary on our last session. Hopefully, I will be well enough to see you this week, at least via Zoom.

Now, back to the beginning.

I don't exactly remember the details of our first sessions together, if I'm being honest. I remember wanting to be in the same room with you because it felt safe there. Or, mostly safe. I remember wondering if you were who you seemed to be. I remember thinking you really listened to me. I remember not wanting to do anything that would lead to me having to stop seeing you.

Raubolt's Voice

Trust established through safety has to be proven again and again because that is what has been destroyed or at least severely damaged through abuse – both aggressive (violence) and abandonment (neglect).

I remember some sessions words would gush out of me. I needed you to know all of the abuse I'd experienced as quickly as possible. I felt like there weren't enough minutes in those sessions. I needed to get you caught up so that you could make the pain stop faster. I worried about you being overwhelmed by what I was saying to you but also needing you to comprehend how bad things were for me as a child because very few people seemed to really comprehend what had happened.

Other sessions, I didn't know what to say. I would sit there staring at you, wanting to explain what was happening inside of me but not having the words to tell you. I wished (and sometimes still do) that you could do a Vulcan mind meld because finding the words, creating a language where you could see the world I lived in, felt impossible. Once, when I'd been silent for several moments, you said something about a psychoanalyst who taught that sessions sometimes ended earlier than the standard 50 minutes because the patient was just done. I was mortified because all I wanted was to stay there in your office with you and not have to leave with myself to walk around the world alone with my memories.

Do you remember those sessions when I couldn't find words? It seems impossible to believe now, because I can fill hours full and still have more to say.

One thing I'd figured out by the time I met you is that very few people can comprehend the depth of trauma my brother and I experienced in childhood.

Raubolt's Voice

Rebecca, as you know, my personal history is much different from yours. With that said, no one is immune from trauma; it is a matter of degree and severity. I felt, and still feel, that I could use my own experiences to enter your world. I have learned, and continue to learn with increasing depth, from those that I see in therapy. Your pain, from the start, moved me. Rather than pushing me away from feeling it and that you were "too much," your history drew me closer. I could see and feel the terrified child in the adult sitting across from me.

It is one thing for people to know that I had been sexually abused by my step-father and two step-brothers beginning at the age of 4 and ending at age 12. But to know that there was also significant physical abuse and a great deal of emotional/psychological manipulation creates a hopelessness for most people. It's hard for people to imagine a house where the parents would take their children to nudist camps, and insist these children not wear clothes in the house. It becomes even more overwhelming to realize that these children were photographed in sexually provocative ways. That other people would come to the house to be photographed in the nude. That a large picture of the children's nude mother hung over the parents' bed.

Worse for some people is the idea that there wasn't any other family to buffer the wounds left by these events. Our biological father, shrouded behind his substance use, was occasionally violent when angry. Our grandmother experienced psychosis and had threatened to kill us when psychotic; our grandfather was present but did not stop the things that were happening.

Raubolt's Voice

The intergenerational nature of violence, chaos, and mental illness left you with no reliable, emotionally stable, responsive adults to guide and protect. The "protectors" were the "persecutors," leaving you not only alone but unable to shield yourself or influence them.

And because of this absence, we would go on to allow so many other people to do so many things to us. I would be sexually abused by other men; I would "have an affair" with a teacher when I was in the eighth grade. I'd been in so many emotionally abusive relationships.

I'd realized by the time I met you that most people needed, for their own well-being, to place me into a category of some kind. For most, once they know about the depth of the traumas I'd experienced, I am settled into the "poor, sad victim" category. This category felt/feels like a way for well-meaning people to distance themselves from me and my trauma. They say to themselves that things like that happen to "those other sad people" they can feel a distant compassion for. It sort of feels like a force field of sorts is built between me and one of these people. These people tend to call me "such a survivor" and "so strong" while subtly distancing themselves.

Another, harder, and less common category that I would find myself put into has been that of "wanting attention" with the possibility that I "was exaggerating" about how bad things were. I believe that this categorization happens when people psychologically cannot handle that the things like what happened to me and my brother actually happen to children. I believe the dissonance of realizing that the child down the street, or the child at church, or the child sitting across from them in some restaurant experiences regular sexual exploitation.

Raubolt's Voice

Rebecca, what you write is true enough. I also believe that it is true that some, perhaps many, abused children seek attention and can do so dramatically. When language is stripped of meaning, offering no protection, when actions are beyond words for many adults, how are children and adults describing their childhood experiences supposed to communicate the betrayals and terror they suffered? What is lacking is not in the "telling" but in hard-edged, skeptical "hearing" that demands consistency, a detailed storyline, and a restrained emotional description; all of which are often distorted or damaged by the very abuse they are trying to reveal.

One alternative possible reason a person would want to put people like me into this "wanting attention/exaggerating" category may be related to either their own denial of their traumas or their participation in harming someone else. I've noticed that abusers tend to downplay the impact of abuse, and so it may be that the people who deny the stories of those of us with severe trauma are deflecting their own participation in or complicity with abuse.

The most painful category I've found myself in once I've revealed my trauma history is that of "damaged beyond repair." This one is used mostly by clinicians, in my opinion. Here is where a personality disorder label is used, the clinical way of saying, "This person isn't likely going to make much progress" or "This person is going to be really difficult to handle."

Raubolt's Voice

I knew your trauma-pain had to be faced, and if therapy were to be helpful, I would need to step into the memories with you. I can never be successful as a therapist if I stay detached, clinical, and unemotional. I don't think anyone can, but I know diagnostic labeling of someone as "untreatable" most often means the therapist is blaming the patient for their own fear of helplessness. Because the work can be challenging and emotionally unsettling for the therapist, there is still no valid therapeutic reason not to try – so often, in trying, the impossible becomes possible. It can just take longer.

It is my belief that it is necessary for the therapist to step into the heart of the patient. With greater specificity, it is necessary to step into the heart that carries the wounds requiring treatment. This is accomplished by listening to (and for) the uninterrupted and unattended cries for help and to dream the undreamt (nightmares) of the patient. Without this profoundly felt, yet not articulated, immersion in the "memories of suffering," there can be no mutual attachment, which in turn prohibits change from becoming transformative.

Having participated in hundreds of clinical consultation meetings and known even more psychotherapists, I know how easily people like me are placed in this category. How calling someone "a borderline" is thrown around whenever people with complex trauma don't respond quickly to therapy. And, I have to tell you, it is extremely painful to witness people I respect doing this. Yet, I have to admit that I've participated in this "label to distance" behavior, too, particularly when I was a younger, more frightened clinician.

I'm not trying to shame anyone for placing me or people like me into a category in order to digest the severity of my trauma. I am trying to give context to where I was when I met you.

The irony is that I have placed myself in every one of these categories at some point. In fact, I have attacked myself with much more destructive categories than those named here. I've noticed every one of my personality flaws and magnified them in ways much more creative than any on-looker could possibly imagine.

I suppose I've done this to protect myself from the imagined barrage of judgmental comments I believe will come my way. I've tried to keep myself protected by inflicting the worst possible damage so that someone else wouldn't happen by and surprise me with their slicing comments. I've remembered and filed away every time I was less than. Less than kind to someone, less than understanding with my son, less than thoughtful in my friendships, and less than enough for my patients. I file away the ways that I can become needy and empty and bruised as evidence of my brokenness.

When I met you, I regularly had severe panic attacks. They began in childhood and were debilitating and embarrassing. I didn't know why they'd happen and couldn't seem to make them stop. Other kids would call me "cry-baby Becky." Teachers would sometimes accuse me of "wanting attention." One teacher actually mocked me in front of all of my peers when I had one in his class. As I got older, they persisted. I had them in college classrooms, in conversations with friends. I once had one in the middle of a work meeting and didn't know how to stop it, so I just sat there sobbing and hiccuping while they continued the meeting. The next day I was told my contract with them was terminated.

These panic attacks would happen when I was overwhelmed or angry or afraid. I wouldn't be able to speak without sobbing. This was not simply crying. It was full-body sobbing. Hiccuping. Hyperventilating. My heart pounding. Sweat covering my back, running down my neck. I couldn't breathe.

Raubolt's Voice

Rebecca, when we first met, feelings of any kind were either mysterious or terrifying to you. One of the most damaging effects of trauma comes from seeing adults, who are to be caretakers, out of control. So often, emotions in these relationships are, to use the common parlance, enacted rather than regulated. Hesitation to allow for reflection goes unacknowledged, replaced instead by an "addiction to action." And since feelings can change so rapidly, the world, your world, became unpredictable and dangerous. There was, from the beginning, a fierce ambivalence about being known, and risking loss, or silence, and risking isolation. At least, that is how I came to see the physical symptoms you describe. Since feelings could not be safely recognized and expressed, they came out intensely and painfully through physical symptoms, which we then had to "unpack."

I also could barely eat. I could go for days without eating much of anything. I'd mostly subsist on cereal and cheese-covered tortillas. Most foods bothered me in some way. I could not eat rice. I could not eat eggs. The texture of both of these foods reminded me of aspects of my sexual abuse. Anything with an unfamiliar smell or taste upset my stomach. I remember telling you that I wished I didn't have to eat because it was so difficult.

Raubolt's Voice

Rebecca, yes, I remember this struggle, too. I believe you had very short hair (shaved?) and loose-fitting clothes that gave me the impression you were hiding in them rather than wearing them. I didn't think there was a question of gender identity as much as there was a wish to be asexual in searching for a safe place to be. During these "early days," you watched me closely and listened carefully, which in turn led me to pay attention to your words, but especially to any non-verbal cues indicating what you may have been feeling. I recall being aware that any comment I might make needed to be carefully considered. I wanted to give neither the appearance, nor experience, of being intrusive or controlling.

When I met you, I wasn't sure people remembered me after they were no longer with me. I was nearly certain that I disappeared for most people when I left the room. I was certain that if they did remember me, they didn't like me anymore.

When I met you, I was certain that I constantly smelled bad. No matter how often I showered, I thought everyone could smell the odor one of my mother's boyfriends said I emanated. He said being around my brother and me caused him to feel ill.

Raubolt's Voice

It is interesting to hear you say this about smelling when my experience of you was so different. I remember thinking you had no personal smell I could detect. Instead, there was an earnest, freshly scrubbed face, sometimes sullen and worried, sometimes hinting, but not fully revealing, how difficult it was to just sit still with me. It was like you were trying to live your days without leaving a trace. I recall feeling that in order to be helpful, I needed to adjust to your pace, move slowly, and above all, be as predictable and consistent as I could manage.

When I met you, I was certain that I would be dead before I made it to 40. In fact, I was somewhat surprised to have made it all the way to 28. I would hear voices talking about my death. One would say, "What happened to her?" The response would be, "She killed herself." Just those two sentences. Nothing else.

I wasn't going to tell you about those voices, though, because I was determined to never return to a psychiatric facility. I'd decided I would die before I'd allow someone to lock me into another hospital. I remember being so relieved when I realized you weren't interested in putting me into the hospital, either.

When I met you, I was desperate. Part of me was certain that I could, in fact, get better if only someone could help point me in a direction. A part of me actually believed it was important that I find my way out of where I'd come from. I held onto a very strong sense that I was supposed to be okay because I had some important mission to complete. This belief is what kept me from giving up – I had to survive, because if I didn't, something important wouldn't get accomplished.

But, when I met you, parts of me were also certain I was beyond repair. That it was just a matter of time before you, too, would know that I was a shattered person. That I was broken. And, worse, that I was despicable and needed to be avoided at all costs.

Yet, from the beginning, you have refused to align with the parts of me that have wanted to prove to you that I could not be fixed, that I am someone so broken that there is no hope. You have continuously refused to label me with a personality disorder.

Raubolt's Voice

Rebecca, I remember one of our early 'disagreements,' or at least differences that stretched our initial alliance, was my refusal to diagnose you as borderline (BPD). You didn't trust me to respond to you differently than the way you were treated when you were hospitalized.

I don't know how aggressively I said it to you, but I certainly felt that in-patient treatment was unwarranted and the diagnosis was wrong. Complex trauma can result in behaviors that appear to reflect personality disorders. This is one of the primary limitations of therapies that focus exclusively on behavioral change. Complex trauma is distinctly different in origin and, in my opinion, needs to be treated much differently, as well.

And, from the beginning, you've listened to the parts of me that long to heal, to connect to others, to have mutual relationships with others. From the beginning, I could feel that you saw the child in me longing to be understood and heard and cared about. It was one of the most relieving and terrifying things back then, because I feared it would disappear without warning. That's what I remember most about the beginning – knowing that someone was willing to be right there with me for the long haul and the fear that it was a dream, an illusion that would disappear. For me, it all started and continues with one constant – showing up.

Raubolt's Voice

I was confident that as I was seeing you I was also reading you to guide how I responded. There were times, though, when I felt the best I could offer you was my presence, my interest, and my willingness to serve as your witness.

Chapter 2

Attaching

Part One

Here's What I've Learned About How Healthy Attachment in Childhood Is Formed

When a child is in distress, they learn through interactions with their caregivers that they can go to the caregiver and receive comfort and/or help when they're distressed. This access to help and comfort is, for the most part, consistently available. The child can be pretty sure that their needs will be met, if not right away, within a reasonable time. If the caregiver misses the child in some way (isn't available right away or becomes frustrated initially), there's usually some kind of repair in their relationship.

When the child no longer needs the caregiver, in a healthy attachment dyad, the caregiver lets the child go. And, as the child goes about their independence, they can look back and know that the caregiver will be there when needed.

Here's What I've Learned Can Go Wrong in Childhood Attachment

When a child is in distress and the caregiver isn't available, the child is left to figure out how to soothe herself. In my mind, she has to make up a story about why no one is there and is left feeling unwanted or perhaps even not real.

Raubolt's Voice

Rebecca, you have anticipated Stolorow (2007) in this regard. He has forcefully argued,

> It cannot be overemphasized that injurious childhood experiences in and of themselves need not be traumatic or pathogenic, provided that they occur within a responsive milieu. Pain is not pathology. It is the absence of adequate attunement and responsiveness to the child's painful emotional reactions that render them unendurable and thus a source of traumatic states of psychopathology.
>
> (p.10)

DOI: 10.4324/9781003604723-2

Or, conversely, when the child wants to leave, when she's gotten what she needs, the caregiver won't let her go. In my mind, the caregiver clings to the child, suffocating her, giving her the sense that she isn't safe out there in the world without the caregiver.

The most dangerous type of attachment occurs when the caregiver chaotically responds to the child's attachment needs. With these caregivers, the child is left uncertain about what to expect. Sometimes, the caregiver is available to the child. Sometimes, they cannot be bothered. Sometimes, they cling to the child. Sometimes, they won't even acknowledge the child. Sometimes, they hit the child, scream at the child, and accuse the child of taking too much, of needing too much. Sometimes, they will push so far into the child's space the child isn't sure there is a separation at all.

Raubolt's Voice

Then, there is the attachment pattern common to children suffering from neglect and abuse (especially sexual abuse). Abusive adults respond to these children by hijacking their needs for love and affection to meet their own wishes. What is a normal developmental need for tenderness, born of innocence, becomes corrupted to serve the narcissistic desires of adult caregivers. Tenderness is distorted and re-defined as passion, leaving the child vulnerable and confused. We have come to refer to this process as a "confusion of tongues" (Ferenczi, 1988). There is not only the loss of physical safety; there is also the loss of language or at least the loss of trust that emotional/physical needs can be effectively expressed or responded to using words.

So, when there's been a healthy attachment, the child can seek help when she needs it and can leave when the help is no longer needed. When attachment isn't healthy, the child either can't get help or can't get away from the help. Or there's chaos – no help, then too much help, then no help again.

Raubolt, what do you think? Did I miss something in that description?

Raubolt's Voice

Rebecca, as you know, attachment begins in infancy. Winnicott (1992) was famous for, among other quotable summations, reminding us there is no baby. He meant, of course, that the infant cannot exist alone but is rather a part of a relationship. Beyond survival, the baby requires consistent, sensitive, and responsive care to develop empathy, empowerment, and resilient self-worth. As is summarized in Emmi Pikler's work (2019), the relationship is all. It is a matter of life for the child.

Here's What I Can Say About My Own Childhood Attachment

My mother and father were teenagers when they had me. My father was raised by an abusive, alcoholic father and an extremely passive mother. He spent periods of time living "on the street" because his father would beat him and kick him out of the house. I don't actually know much more than that about my father's life before he met my mother, as I only met his parents a few times and really didn't spend all that much more time with him.

My mother's mother was diagnosed with schizophrenia and spent time in and out of psychiatric facilities. She'd received shock treatments and may have had a lobotomy, but I am not completely sure about that, as my family avoided talking directly about my grandmother's mental health concerns. Based on my professional training and my observation of her, I would guess my grandmother actually had a mood disorder with psychosis and not schizophrenia. Whatever the diagnosis, she was volatile and frightening. Both of my mother's parents were alcoholics, though they reacted to the alcohol in very different ways. The times that I saw my grandmother drunk were the times she'd become psychotic. I was too young to know whether it was the alcohol that triggered the psychosis or the psychosis that led her to drink.

My mother would sometimes drop my brother and me at my grandmother's house so we "would know what a hard life actually is." I remember my grandmother chasing us through her apartment screaming because my brother touched the telephone and now the government would know what we were doing. If she caught us, she would hit us. I remember her on top of my brother, hitting him repeatedly.

My grandfather was a funnier, happier drunk. But he was also not around to help protect his children, and he didn't protect my brother and me when we needed him. When my mother was a child, he would periodically live in her house, but he mostly lived with another woman and her family. According to one of my aunts, he would return to my grandmother long enough to get her pregnant and then leave her and the children alone for years at a time. This meant that my mother and her siblings were mostly left to be raised by their psychotic mother.

When my parents got pregnant with me, they got married. Both were rejected by their families and left to fend for themselves. According to both of them (told to me at different points in my childhood), my father began beating my mother pretty early in their marriage. He pushed her down the stairs when she was pregnant with my brother. I have a very vivid memory of my father bragging to another man about beating my mother to the point of putting her into the hospital because her purse strap tangled with his camera strap, causing his camera to fall when she grabbed her purse.

I am explaining all of this history to give context to how things were when I was born. So much of what I know comes from my mother, who is, at best, a questionable historian, and from my memories.

One of my first memories, and the only memory of my parents living together, is of being in what must have been a highchair, trying to get my mother's attention as my father screamed at her. I don't remember anything more about that moment; just wanting her attention and him yelling. After that, all of my memories of my parents are from after their divorce. They divorced when I was 3.

Before the age of 4, I have memories of my mother singing to my brother and me. I remember her cleaning and cleaning and cleaning. I have memories of her sitting on our couch glassy-eyed and smoking what I now know was marijuana. I remember having to move to different houses often and different men living with us, one who was very kind. I remember I was to take care of my brother and not get upset about anything.

Raubolt's Voice

Rebecca, you're describing the three major characteristics supporting what I have come to call "pathogenic normalcy." First, when there is a history of unmetabolized intergenerational trauma, a family can develop a culture of denial: dangerous, violent behavior is excused, minimized, rationalized, or misrepresented as necessary. Secondly, this, in turn, is entwined with significant individual pathology (as was the case with your grandmother) although not commonly of a psychotic nature, instead narcissistic and/or paranoid personality disorders dominate the clinical picture (as was the case with your father). Additionally, there is the likelihood of a concomitant pattern of substance abuse, usually excessive alcohol consumption, if not alcoholism, and the presentation of anti-social and violent proclivities.

When I was about 4 and a half, my mother met a man who would become my stepfather. His name was Bob, and he was a photographer. The story I was told was that they met when he was photographing her.

Bob was, and still is, an anomaly to me. He was from Boston, and he'd been to college. He was well-read, at least, I was under the impression that he was because there were always books in his house, something very different from the houses I'd lived in before he came into our lives and after he'd left.

I know this story is an important one to you, Raubolt, because you've brought it up several times over the years. The story of the first time I'd met Bob.

He came over to the house where we were staying. It must have been evening, because I remember being in a nightgown. I had my first wiggly tooth. He came with a little white purse which held a little tube of lipstick and, I think, little white gloves. I remember feeling special and pretty because he'd made lots of comments about how beautiful my hair and eyes were. You've said that was the beginning of his grooming me, and I know you're right, but for some reason, it is difficult for me to sit with that truth. Because it was the first time I felt like anyone really liked me.

Raubolt's Voice

Rebecca, I know it has been painful to "lose" this memory as fond and gentle. You are right – I see Bob's behavior as predatory, manipulative, and strategic. To my mind, he exploited the volatile and unstable atmosphere your mother created by presenting illusionary responsiveness, stability, and safety. He could and would routinely build you up with compliments on your intelligence while tearing you down for any physical flaw he believed you had. Then, he would photograph you through a sexual lens, spreading to all interactions with him, while also only supporting your mother's influence as it aligned with his, completing a suffocating and dangerous cycle of violence.

That's what I know about my early attachment. I felt mostly unseen, for the most part an annoyance to my mother. She would be tender at times, but mostly, she was irritated with my brother and me. I remember she'd change into an entirely different person whenever there was a man around. I remember thinking she was the most beautiful person in the world, and I remember loving her with my entire being but feeling like I wasn't good enough for her.

And, my father. I remember seeing him every so often, knowing that it scared my mother when he'd show up. Later, I learned that we moved so often because she was hiding from my father. And, then he'd show up, and we would move. Later, we would have to see him, be around him. He would shift between being emotional and weeping because he missed us so much and becoming angry and violent for an unknowable reason. I remember him hitting my brother so hard, while hanging onto one of his arms, that my brother's body lifted off the ground. I don't remember him hitting me, but I would guess that is either because I've forgotten it happening or because I had already figured out how to be as small and quiet as I could when I noticed my father's moods had turned. It is most likely the latter, but I honestly don't know.

So, when Bob arrived on the scene, I was starved emotionally, and he was all too ready to feed me his poison.

Raubolt's Voice

Poison disguised as candy.

That sounds so dramatic.

Raubolt's Voice

I don't see how you could ever overstate the danger he posed. Do I now risk sounding overly dramatic?

I know, but that's how I understand what happened and what I was willing to do in order to feel loved by him. But, his attention was inconsistent, too. Sometimes, I would feel like I was important and special to him. He would comment on my looks, telling me that I could be a model because I was so beautiful, only to make fun of my body at another time, calling me "big butt Becky" or saying that the flaws on my face (the fact that my nose was uneven) were going to make it very difficult to be a model. He would tell me that I was brilliant, that I could go to college if I wanted to, only to later tell me that I thought too much of myself, that I didn't seem to catch on very quickly.

Bob also separated me from others by comparing me to them. When I was very young, he would compare my intelligence to that of my brother and then later to my mother. He compared my body to my mother's body when I was a bit older. He compared me to an aunt, making comments regarding his hope that I would never "get that fat."

Raubolt, I'm going to tell you a little about what happened when I got to this part of the narrative about attachment. Until this point, I'd been writing pretty easily. The topic wasn't pleasant, but the words were flowing fairly easily. Secretly, I'd wanted to be able to complete the entire chapter before sending it to you, because I wanted to show that I was feeling sure of myself and this process. In the last chapter, I'd had to send it to you after writing only a few pages because I needed reassurance that I could say all of what I wanted to say. This time, I'd wanted to show you – more likely show me – that I could do this independently and was not in any way needy.

But, then I got to the last paragraph in which I was describing how I could never trust anything about myself when dealing with Bob – how he would give and take and give and take. I'd become nauseous, like I was on a boat in the middle of a squall. I stopped writing then, thinking I could come back to it, but still wanting to forge on my own until the end of the chapter. Twenty-four hours passed, during which I could have written but nothing, then 48 hours. Then, while I was minding my own business, reading a novel, I was haunted by the sexual abuse by one of my stepbrothers. (I call it a haunting and not a flashback because I no longer experience the all-encompassing-take-over of my mind that happened when I had active flashbacks. Instead, it now feels like the ghosts of the past remind me of their existence, but I am not lost in the scenes from which they were born).

I then knew I could not move forward without sending you what I'd written and sent it off. It bothers me that I needed your assurance. Yet, it is also a reminder to myself that to be attached to another is to allow them to help when I'm distressed and not a sign of being needy or wanting too much.

I will return to the narrative of my early experiences of attachment.

I believe I attached more to Bob than I had to either of my parents, and this attachment is one of the reasons I psychologically/emotionally survived. And, this attachment was also the most damaging to my being. What I mean by the idea that it saved me is that Bob actually paid attention to me. By the time he came into my life, my mother was either working or cognitively checked out. I hadn't seen much of my father, other than his showing up randomly, causing my mother to become upset. We had various babysitters, one of whom was wonderful but inconsistent in my life. Most of the others didn't really want my brother and me there – we were a source of income but not a source of interest. I was so hungry for any kind of acknowledgment of my being alive that had I not received any attention for much longer, I believe I would have dulled, my light extinguished.

Raubolt's Voice

Rebecca, writing as you do about Bob demonstrates one of the topics I struggled with most to achieve some type of therapeutic balance; colloquially, when he was good, he could be very good to you, but when he was bad, he could be brutal. I knew I needed to recognize the gift of attention and belief in you that he brought into your life. I also knew he was monstrously effective in neutralizing any protective restraints expected of adults where children are concerned. I could see how he hid his intentions and disguised his violence in the normalcy he was playing upon through compliments and expectations for academic success. Just because I could see it didn't mean I should say it, not all of it, anyway. To say too much too soon could risk threatening our still new, fragile relationship. To say nothing, on the other hand, could appear to place me among those adults who took no notice of your suffering.

Yet, despite it saving my life, attaching to him also meant that he was able to leave a lasting damage that is hard to repair. Because I attached more to him than anyone else, he had so much more say over the development of my personhood than either of my biological parents. His is the voice I hear most often, the one that integrated into my own voice, so that his judgments and comparisons live in me. His inconsistent message of my worth is the source of my inconsistent sense of self.

I had another long-term therapist before I met you, Raubolt. Her name was Julie, and she saw me for about five years after I was discharged from the hospital. I attached to her, deeply. She was funny and kind, and she listened closely to what had happened to me. I would think about her and wonder about what she would think about things between sessions. Some days, she was the only thing keeping me tethered to the planet. To be honest, I became kind of obsessed with her. I wanted to know where she lived, what her life was like, and whether she cared about me. Once, when I was on a walk, she drove past me and turned into a house about three blocks from my apartment. From that day forward, I would walk past that house whenever I felt upset or afraid. I never knew whether she lived in that house, but I held onto the belief that she was in there, and this gave me a modicum of relief on the days when being alive meant being in unending pain.

I experienced a lot of shame regarding this obsession with Julie, because I knew it wasn't how I was supposed to act. I knew that she would likely think I was stalking her and that this would mean she would stop seeing me. This was before social media existed, but if it had at that time, I would have done everything I could to find out as much as I possibly could about her.

My therapy with her ended when I moved out of the state. This was long before telehealth, and the option to practice across state lines existed. It was difficult to leave treatment with her, and when I returned to Michigan less than six months later, I tried to contact her to restart. Sadly, when I tried to restart with her, I learned she was no longer practicing but had become a landscape designer. Later, I would learn that the reason for this change in career was because she had an affair with a client and her license was revoked.

Learning about her relationship with another client shook me. By this time, I was a practicing clinician and knew the number one rule taught in every ethics class in every branch of mental health: don't sleep with your client. So, I was scandalized that this person I trusted so fully would break such a basic rule. But, there was another feeling, one that struck to the core of my being. Why didn't she pick me to love? Why didn't she care that much about me? Of course, I don't even know if she cared for this other person. I hope she did. But, because love and care by a person in some kind of authority role were mixed up with sex already for me, I felt queasy with confusion about the entire idea. Another attachment figure distorting the idea of care.

Raubolt's Voice

Rebecca, as you note, a sexual tryst between therapist and patient is a primary violation of ethical behavior and decency. Therapists can go wrong, very wrong, in misreading the nature of strong feelings of affection laced with erotic expression. Sex, even if described as willing, is not mutual because the therapist is rarely, if ever, the true object of desire. He or she is a "stand in," a transference figure, where old childhood scripts are evoked and acted upon. These feelings are distinctly different from loving, tender feelings that can arise when safety is established through attention and consistency. Therapists are responsible for maintaining protective, flexible boundaries. By this, I mean that not only must they refrain from acting on their own feelings of attraction, they also need to address and contain emerging sexual inklings on the part of patients. It must be recalled that patients who have been abused sexually come to treatment with experiences where sex, violence, betrayal, seduction, tenderness, and physical soothing have formed a volatile mix. If the therapist responds to what is believed to be a desire for physical intimacy, they egregiously violate professional conduct and destroy the safety needed for curiosity, exploration, imagination, and reverie – the stuff of therapy. Adults are not to have sex with children, nor are therapists to have sex with adults under their care. One last comment here. The actions of your former therapist, although not directly expressed in your treatment, had reverberations that continued in your therapy with me.

The beginning of my attachment to you, Raubolt, was filled with extreme fear and intense longing. In some ways, I immediately attached. Yet, looking back, I think that may have not been actual attachment but instead the precursor to it. I don't know if anyone has ever talked about this idea, but I've observed both personally and professionally that there is first a desire to attach, an attraction to the other that may be a combination of projection and wish. It sort of reminds me of a crush, of infatuation. Whether that attraction becomes actual attachment is unknown at this stage.

Raubolt's Voice

Rebecca, if the process you describe is activated, then it is a good sign attachment will develop. There must be enough social hunger, capacity to consider and reflect, and basic trust despite any emotional damage sustained in order to form a working/therapeutic relationship. The wish to attach, accompanied by either infatuation or projection, can serve as the initial footing in establishing a positive transference. This beginning can be hopeful and yet exquisitely painful because in seeking a connection (loving connection?), prior feelings of betrayal, abandonment, and deceit can, and most often do emerge. Psychodynamic therapy or psychoanalysis moves back and forth, in and out of transference and a new, real relationship.

Since I can hardly improve on the words of one of my teachers, Antonio Coimbra de Matos (2009), let me quote him:

> The patient comes to us with a story, or rather, with many stories to tell us. With the material of those old stories, we build a new story – one that begins in our therapy, in our new relationship – and this new story is the legitimate child of an authentic analytic relationship. It entails a new style of relationship that is more open, deeper and more expansive in its progressive relevance to the patient's daily life.
>
> (p. xv)

And, to highlight coming theoretical discussions, this new relationship entails "the touching of souls" (de Matos). Over time, a felt sense or experience develops that may be described as, "I feel that you feel what I feel. What that is, I don't know; but I know that you feel what I feel."

Fairly early into our work together, you'd referred me to a psychiatrist to help with the all-encompassing depression and terror I was experiencing. His initial assessment took significantly longer than expected, and I was scheduled to see you, across an unfamiliar town (we'd only moved to Grand Rapids a short time before I started seeing you). I tried to end the intake with the psychiatrist, telling him, "I'm going to be late for my therapy with Dr. Raubolt." To which he responded, "What you're doing with me is much more important than what you'd be doing with him."

When he finally released me, I had to call you because I was already late and I didn't know how to get to your office (the world before GPS). I was sobbing because I knew I wouldn't have my whole time with you and because I believed I was failing you in some way. You talked with me for most of my ride to your office as I sobbed, assuring me that you would be there when I arrived. That I would be okay and that it was alright to feel angry and afraid.

Raubolt's Voice

Rebecca, this was one of those times I had to modulate my feelings in order to respond effectively to you. I don't know how much I expressed at the time, I suspect very little, but I was furious at the reaction the psychiatrist displayed to your plight. His arrogance and inflated self-importance were not only unprofessional, they also created harm by intensifying your anxiety in a dismissive, condescending manner. Whatever his intention was, I do not know, but I do know I read his words as misunderstanding and undermining the transference. A decade-plus after hearing those words of his, I remain incredulous.

For me, in that first stage of treatment, it felt like my world revolved around our sessions. I thought about you all of the time, and I sincerely hated any disruption to the treatment. But, I was also angry that you had so much impact on me. I hated the way I'd feel after each session. It was as though my guts were hanging out, exposed to the elements, and I would be left alone to spoon them back into myself. And, I loved and hated you for it.

One thing I now realize is that I was attracted to you, to some extent, because you reminded me of Bob. Or, at least, the Bob he wanted all of us to believe in. He portrayed himself as a learned, sophisticated man. He was always dressed much better than most of the men in my world at the time. I grew up in mostly industrial areas where men were either unemployed or worked in factory settings or drove semi-trucks. Bob was "white collar," my mother once explained to me. He wore slacks and a collared shirt. He was well-spoken.

Similarly, you have always dressed well, Raubolt. Even when you've worn more casual clothes, they're high-end and stylish. Psychotherapists are not usually as well dressed – usually preferring to look like college professors in sweaters and jeans. And, you were obviously well-educated, sophisticated. Your offices (I've seen you in three different places!) have all been furnished with tasteful, expensive furniture. You also had these statues that reminded me of Bob and the houses we lived in while he was in our lives.

Bob was obsessed with nudity. There's no other way of describing this. There was the drawing of my mother's nude body that I mentioned earlier. He had a "stress ball" shaped like a breast. In the summer, he would insist that we not wear clothes in the house in the evenings. He took us to nudist camps and hit me when I wanted to keep my shirt on. He said wearing underwear under our pajamas was unhygienic. He had books and magazines and statues of nude figures from Africa.

Your statues were not as graphic as the ones Bob had, but looking at them those first years would make me wonder if you, too, were obsessed with nudity, if you, too, thought about how everyone looked without clothes. Do you remember the day I yelled at you for those statues? It was some time into our treatment. You were in your second office, so it must have been more than two years in. I'd been staring at them – the shapes of African women in wood with the large breasts – for so long, and suddenly, I exploded about them. I don't remember exactly what I said, but I know I had begun accusing you of being like Bob, I think. What do you remember? All I know is that they were gone the following session, and I felt simultaneously ashamed of my anger and relieved that I didn't have to see them.

Raubolt's Voice

Rebecca, yes, I remember the exchanges you described. My recollection of the details is different. I did have two small African figures that were much smaller than statue-size in my mind. One was "flat-chested," and the other did have breasts that were proportionally sized. Until you brought it to my attention, I did not view them as sexually provocative – once you did, I decided to explore your reactions since they were so closely embedded in your history with Bob. I also decided that I would remove them. I thought it would be difficult, perhaps not even possible, to explore any transference implications when there was a real-time stimulus (the figures) generating anxiety. To me, they were, until that time, art that was tastefully crafted. What I came to see through your confrontation was the ubiquitous sexual milieu you grew up with and my insensitivity to this reality. Since "they" risked creating undue and unnecessary harm, I saw to it that they were removed before your next appointment. As I recall, this incident was the first time you forcefully and angrily challenged me. Removing the "statutes" established some emotional room for you to experience your anger as influential and powerful. I did not apologize, fearing this could be viewed as a manipulative ploy serving to mute your reactions and lessen my anxiety. Taking them from the room was my way of acknowledging your feelings and allowing us the context to unpack the experience both historically and in real, present time. To my mind, there are two basic ways to address this clinical dilemma: the traditional way, i.e., continue to verbally explore the internal fantasies related to the external object that provoked pain and suffering (the cause of which was already explored and could/would continue to be explored in the future); OR, in a new and different fashion i.e., actually attending to the *old and internal uninterrupted cries for help* by transforming reality first and then expecting internal transformations (instead of hoping for the other way around). An example from another treatment as described by Diaz (Diaz, J. P., personal communication, March 2, 2023) may be useful here:

> I am reminded of a session where my patient was lying on the couch, talking about her fear of her mother and suddenly she saw a relatively small spider crossing the wall next to her. She froze with dread. Without thinking, I stepped up, walked towards the wall, crushed it, and said: "Sorry little one, but you're bothering both of us"; then, I went back to my place and we continued discussing what we were talking about, without referring to the "incident."

Months later, she reported back that she was relieved that at that time, I didn't make any comments about her "fearful reaction" – as her mother used to do (humiliating her by highlighting her fragility), or any interpretation about a possible mother-spider connection (as her husband, a psychologist, usually did); most importantly, she said she felt because I continued to focus on what she was saying before the spider appeared, I was not "showing her" how "strong I was," nor how she "should behave."

The bottom line is that the therapist must continuously attempt to respond to the patient's needs in a way that:

1) Feels alive, real, and beneficial for both of them.
2) Creates and reinforces a sense of we-ness between them.
3) Transfers his sense of power, strength, and knowledge to the patient as naturally and smoothly as possible.

4) Allows the patient to empower and acknowledge herself for her own achievements (by remaining as much as possible humbly behind but firmly supportive of the patient's progressions).

In those first sessions, all I wanted was your approval. Well, if I'm being honest, I also wanted you to love me. Perhaps that's true for many patients with a new therapist, but it seemed to me that my life depended on it. I seemed to be tilting in and out of reality during those sessions, giving you glimpses of myself and then wanting to hide away from you lest you see too much and tell me I had to go.

I believe the main reason I finally let go and began to attach was because of, in all of those wild days, your genuine kindness. You gently reassured me even when I yelled at you about the statues and sobbed in my car because I couldn't get to you on time. In your patience and care, you offered me the opportunity for something new. As Ferenczi wrote regarding there being any hope of "a different outcome from the original trauma, then the victim of traumatic shock must be offered something in reality, at least as much caring attention, or a genuine intention to provide it, as a severely child must have" (p. 28).

References

De Matos, A. C. (2009). *Touching of Souls*. Unpublished manuscript, Portugal.

Ferenczi, S. (1988). *The Clinical Diary of Sándor Ferenczi*. Edited by J. Dupont. Translated by M. Balint and N. Z. Jackson. Harvard University Press.

Pikler, E. (2019). *The Pikler Approach: A Parenting Guide*. Translated by P. W. L. Murray. Routledge.

Stolorow, R. D. (2007). *Trauma and Human Existence: Autobiographical, Psychoanalytic, and Philosophical Reflections*. Routledge.

Winnicott, D. W. (1992). Metapsychological and clinical aspects of regression within the psychoanalytic set up. In D. W. Winnicott, *Through Paediatics to Psychoanalysis, Collected Papers* (2nd ed., pp. 228–249). Karnac Books.

Chapter 3

Attaching
Part Two

Those early years of treatment were difficult and confusing and full of ambivalence for me. Some days, I loved you, Raubolt, with this sort of painful longing that took my breath away; others, I resented how much I wanted to see you. I couldn't quite believe you to be a real person, so I would dismiss your kindness as an act.

In a 2003 journal entry, I wrote:

> *Psychotherapy is such a mysterious endeavor even for those of us who practice it. One day a person is wreaking havoc on themselves and others in their life. The next day they understand and change. Because of a relationship, one that is unique to all others. One that gives more and gives less at the same time.*
>
> *Raubolt. What to say of him with his quiet speech and gentleness. He is my dream father. And my confessor. Yet, I know nothing of him or what he truly thinks of me. And that is both frightening and assuring. To love and despise so deeply another person who is only really an illusion brought on by my longing, by my transference.*

I processed traumas with you, as I had with so many therapists before you. Though I have to admit, you seemed to understand it differently than anyone before you. It didn't feel as though you were punching a therapy card with me, if that makes any sense. Sometimes, with clinicians before you, I felt as though they were punching in for their shift and waiting until they could be done with listening to me.

One of the first adjustments I had to make when I began seeing you was the idea of lying on your couch. The first time I saw the couch, I have to admit I was amused. I'd "grown up" as a clinician in a highly behavioral undergraduate program and what had been called an "eclectic" master's program, which basically meant I had no true theoretical home. In my own practice, I'd integrated some of the cognitive behavioral theories with some behavioral theory with some person-centered theory with some "my idea of what might work" theory. I was still pretty young as a clinician when I met you, having practiced for about five years, but I didn't really realize just how young I was, yet.

What had been drilled into my mind was the idea that psychoanalysis wasn't "real science" and should be avoided at all costs. In fact, in my undergraduate

DOI: 10.4324/9781003604723-3

studies, the professors used psychoanalysis as a punching bag for all things "unmeasurable." Psychoanalysis was synonymous with Freud and was archaic and penis focused. I remember a professor making comments about the irresponsibility of any of us ever even thinking about psychoanalysis (and, by default, psychodynamic therapy) as a viable arena of study.

Raubolt's Voice

Yes, over the years, I have heard such ignorance spouted a number of times. So many supposedly educated academics have failed to do their homework. Lazily, they have failed to recognize how much psychoanalytic theory has changed since Freud to the point that drive theory has lost its place of prominence. The relational approach is now the dominant theory, and psychoanalytic therapy has largely replaced psychoanalysis. This said, concepts such as the unconscious, resistance, transference, countertransference, and acting out remain clinically useful. Newer ideas like embodiment, mentalization, intergenerational trauma, cryptonymy, and enactment, to name a few, have revitalized the field and informed treatment. So, what then are the goals of psychodynamic therapy that your instructors so enjoyed punching but I find so clinically relevant? Which on this admittedly abbreviated list is so objectionable: symptomatic relief, development of insight, increased personal agency, solidifying a sense of identity, improvement in the ability to recognize and regulate feelings, development of resilient self-cohesion, or enhancement of the capacity to love, work and play?

The problem for me was I'd been in behavioral and cognitive behavioral-oriented psychotherapy before. While I did gain some help from these treatments, such as learning relaxation techniques and ways of correcting irrational thoughts, I was mostly left feeling like I'd failed in some way. I couldn't seem to change my thoughts when I was upset or remembering terrible traumas. I continued to have panic attacks and flashbacks. So, I was ready to give psychodynamic/psychoanalysis a try despite all of the negative comments I'd heard about it not being science-based. In all honesty, it was my last ditch effort by the time I'd gotten to see you, Raubolt. I was beginning to believe I wasn't going to feel better.

But lying down on an actual "Freudian" couch? That was a step too far in the beginning. I couldn't imagine how such a thing could be helpful to me, and I needed to see you. Lying down on a couch with a stranger, a strange man, seemed slightly dangerous. You understood. You explained that people found it easier to go deeper, to not get distracted. At least, that's what I remember you saying, but maybe you remember that differently?

Raubolt's Voice

Essentially, yes, that is what I believe I said. Now, outside the clinical hour, I can add a few more comments. The couch need not be restricted to use only for psychoanalysis. Psychotherapists who are aware of the potential for untoward regression and know how to cope with any resulting effects of fragmentation should consider using the couch. I am suggesting, as a rule of thumb, that the decision to use it depends on the indications or contraindications for a particular patient at a particular time. While the trauma you experienced was extensive, you also possessed the ability to observe yourself, experience painful memories, feel the depths of your emotions, and regulate your behavior. I watched and listened for signs of "malevolent regression," but I did not observe any despite the intensity of your memories. Using the couch changed the pace of our interaction by reducing the pressure to speak or engage in any distracting social pleasantries or back-and-forth dialogue. While making more room for you to think, reflect, and remember, it also allowed me space to unwind, let my thoughts wander, and gain access to my unconscious associations and connections.

It didn't happen right away, of course. It took some time for me to give it a go, but I really was pretty desperate by this time. Something about you, the solidness of your convictions that this would help, convinced me. And, so, I did it. I lay on the couch and stared up at the ceiling. I don't remember much about the first office you were in, at McKay Tower, but I remember the second office's ceiling very well. I memorized the tiles of that ceiling, by the way. I knew where there'd been some water damage, where the lights were positioned in relation to the couch. I remember that you worried about the light bothering me and my not wanting to admit that it did because I worried it would disappoint you.

For someone not familiar with lying on the couch, let me explain that it is a completely different experience from sitting across from someone. I will describe it from my perspective, as I imagine it is different for everyone. For me, there was a level of simultaneous intimacy with another and privacy from the other that is difficult to explain. Raubolt, you sat just behind and to the side of me. It was physically closer, I think, than it was when you sat across from me. But, because I couldn't see you, it felt further away until you spoke. When you spoke, your proximity to me made your words feel more intimate and powerful.

Raubolt's Voice

Here might be a good time for me to quote my own analyst, Ernest Wolf (1995), who wrote:

> The position of the analyst, out of sight behind the patient on the couch, is indeed a potent trigger in itself, a trigger the experience of which is largely shaped not only by the patient transferring from the past but also by the uniquely expressed presence of the particular analyst sitting behind the patient.
>
> (p. 316)

I was able to think more about me and less about you most of the time when I was on the couch. I could not watch your face as I did when I sat across from you, which meant I was not scanning for approval or disapproval. I could say things about what had happened without worrying about the pain I saw on your face, and this allowed me to admit to all kinds of feelings. But, it also meant I sometimes felt I faced the memories alone, which pushed me deeper into reliving them. Until your voice, so close by, came and brought me back out again.

You'd suggested that I see you twice a week fairly early into my treatment. It was startling for me. I wondered if you were worried about my vague suicidal thoughts, worried you thought I needed to return to the hospital. But, you said (and still contend) that it was because I was capable of handling a more intense therapy and that it would help move my treatment forward more quickly than would happen in one session per week. I was fairly certain you were giving me some kind of line, some sweetness, so I would agree to a bigger dose of medicine. What you didn't know is that I would have done anything you asked of me if it would help me stop hurting.

Now, years later, I actually believe that both of the reasons you gave me were true. I've now seen that some patients cannot tolerate twice-a-week treatment even if they're in a lot of distress – some very fragile patients become overwhelmed psychologically if they're seen too often. Instead of it being helpful, it can potentially cause too much distress. And, I've recognized with the patients who are able to tolerate that intensity that the therapy does go deeper more rapidly. I've seen that in both my own personal work and the work of my patients, that more frequent sessions allows for the work to go further into reflections because less time is spent reporting events. Raubolt, you could probably articulate this more clearly.

In some ways, the fact that I was capable of doing this deeper work from the beginning surprises me. I felt so fragile, myself, back then. I experienced so many flashbacks, was passively suicidal, was so lost. It scares me sometimes to think of just how much pain I was in then. Yet, it also doesn't surprise me in other ways. I'd been determined to have a different life than the one I'd had up to that point, and something I now appreciate about myself is the level of determination I have.

I also had to get used to seeing a man for therapy. The person I was seeing just before I started seeing you was also a man, but I hadn't seen him for very long and wasn't exactly in treatment with him – I wasn't attached in any way to him. He was a nice person I'd talked to for a few months, but I could not tell him about what had happened in any detail. This was likely because he was talking about when my therapy would end beginning in the first session, and likely, on some level, I couldn't talk with him because he was a man.

I'd sworn I would never again see a man for psychotherapy after the man who'd fallen asleep in my session. I said that I would never be able to relax enough to really discuss what had happened to me with a man. But, a friend who was also a clinician said that if I was afraid of therapy with a man, then I should probably see a man to get over this fear.

I never said this to the friend or really to anyone, but I was fairly certain that a man would use my sexual abuse history against me in some way. Looking back on those feelings, I realize I had a pretty good reason for my caution. I mentioned earlier that a teacher "had an affair" with me when I was in the eighth grade. I quoted "affair" because I now realize that it was not an affair; it was another adult man using my need for help and comfort against me.

I'd told this teacher about my sexual abuse. I wrote him this long letter in which I explained what had happened to me and how much I struggled with my emotions about it. My stepfather, Bob, had moved out only two years earlier, and my mother was unraveling. My brother was beginning to show signs of the mood disorder that would eventually kill him. I needed someone to help me.

That teacher took this need and sexualized it. He would meet me near the train tracks that ran behind my neighborhood. He would encourage me to hide in the wheel well of his car until we were out of the city limits, and he would drive me to a college town about 40 miles away from where I lived for our "dates." Or, I would leave my house at night and walk the two miles to his apartment. My mother was so unconnected to us that she never knew I was gone. This relationship went on for about six months until the teacher told me I was "too emotionally needy" and ended things with me.

So, the act of seeing a man for therapy was, in truth, terrifying. In some ways, it may have also been a way I placed myself into some danger. I may have been trying to relive the abuse. I don't know. It wasn't conscious if I was.

What I didn't know, couldn't have known, was that it turned out to be one of the things that healed me the most. I wish that I could say that I had any insight into what that friend was saying to me years ago. I'd like to say that I understood the idea that I would need to face this group of people who frightened me the most in order to heal something important. But, I didn't see a man for that reason. I listened to that friend mostly because I felt challenged and I was loath to avoid such a challenge. But, I didn't actually believe it would help my fear of men. Yet, it has been this relationship with you that has allowed me to form deep, caring relationships with a few men which have nothing to do with sex or exploitation.

At your encouragement, Raubolt, I'm going to step back for a moment and talk about what it has been like for me to write these last few chapters. To put it plainly, the process has been painfully therapeutic. None of what I've written is new information. I've never really forgotten any of it, so it isn't as though I've unearthed some deep memory that has shaken my reality and created new pain from the discovery. Yet, there has been a reliving of parts of what happened. The other night, I woke my entire household because I was screaming in my sleep. Interestingly, in the dream, I'd warned some unseen person who grabbed me under my arms that if they didn't let go, I would scream. And, I did scream. Something I wouldn't have dared even consider as a child or even a younger adult. So, while the reliving is frightening, it is also a time for me to notice that my voice is strong and that I will scream.

Raubolt's Voice

Rebecca, I agree this is an important dream. Even in the midst of emotionally revisiting the past, you were not constrained by that history. Defending yourself would have been dangerous back then, and screaming would have been silenced when it was a mere whimper. In the dream, you gave a warning and, when it was ignored, you unleashed your protest powerfully and dramatically. You would not go silently into the night.

While writing all of this has not re-traumatized me, it has been painful. There is a re-ordering and a new understanding of some of what has happened. For example, after writing about the experiences with my teacher, you and I had a session during which you commented that this teacher, upon receiving my letter about my abuse, likely used the letter like personal pornography to stimulate himself. This, of course, makes sense and is likely true. And, it left me feeling as though I was punched in the gut, as though I could vomit. Even now, writing this, I feel my stomach tighten and a grief sweep through me for my younger self and for all of the children who have something like this happen to them.

Raubolt's Voice

Rebecca, those who would dismiss psychoanalytic therapy as merely a talking therapy underestimate the power of language. In commenting on the teacher's manipulation(s) I had a few choices, but it came down to what impact I was seeking with my words. Since we had talked about this teacher before, I thought (and felt) I could go deeper in suggesting that the "pornographic ambiance" in your home life was not contained there. Those who seek out children as sexual partners have the uncanny "ability" to prey on them long before the children are aware of what is happening. My words were meant to graphically capture and expose the nature of this type of seduction. While I do not subscribe to the medical model when it comes to the practice of therapy, I do believe words can be used surgically. Considerable clinical judgment is required if and when I decide to cut a little deeper. There are times, and the incident you describe when we discussed this teacher is one of them, where I believe an explanation must be conveyed with emotion. Sometimes, I use my personal reactions, and sometimes, like here, I want a point I am making to stand out against the background. Now, for a moment, I want to step outside my designated role as your therapist and speak candidly as a man. I find the conduct of men like this teacher reprehensible, and I believe further that there is a special place in Dante's Hell for men like him. My challenge with feelings like these is to recognize their presence and to be thoughtful as I give them expression. This teacher not only betrayed the trust expected of an educator, but he took your plea for help, twisted it, and returned it to you even more damaged. It almost broke you, but somehow, your resolve to live better than you were treated survived.

When I was a younger clinician, I was told that people who had multiple episodes of assault likely brought it on themselves. I remember feeling so much shame whenever I'd hear that – usually said by someone who didn't know what I'd been through. The comments weren't meant as blaming, necessarily. They were trying to make sense of the subgroup of traumatized people who had so much more interpersonal trauma than the average person did. They'd noticed that these people didn't seem to "learn from" the original trauma and steer clear of predators.

From my experience, when interpersonal violation happens to a very young person, as did with me, all of the alarm systems in the person get turned off. The child stops recognizing danger or believes they don't have the right to not be used. In my imagination, it's like chefs who no longer feel heat when they reach into an oven. So, it isn't that the child "brings it on themselves." It is that they no longer recognize the fire, the danger.

Saying all of this here has allowed me to explain things to clinicians, both current and future, and this is healing. It feels as though I'm offering compassion to others like me and self-compassion to the clinicians who might have a history like mine. But, I also feel vulnerable and wide open in some ways to the judgment of clinicians who believe people like me shouldn't be in the field.

When I returned to school to earn my doctorate 11 years after I received my Master of Arts, I was confronted with the fact that some of my faculty believed that students with significant trauma histories should not be in the field. Once, I'd begun a conversation with one such faculty member about the fact that therapists often have their own trauma histories, and before I could get to my point (that training programs should help them learn to handle this), the faculty member said, "I know. It's such a problem, but we haven't figured out how to screen them out." This conversation eventually led to my dissertation topic, which I will talk about later in the book, but it also left me under a blanket of shame and fears that maybe I shouldn't be here, that I was damaged beyond repair, that I was functioning above my true ability.

So, as I've written these past few chapters, I've wondered if this book is such a good idea. I've been trying to decide if I should publish under a pen name in order to protect myself from the judgment of such clinicians. I've wondered if this is like the letter I gave to my teacher which led to more abuse. I've wondered if I'm ignoring the fire and will open myself to dangers.

Yet, in this telling, I am not in need of love. I am loved and have created a life so far beyond my childhood comprehension of the possibilities for myself that I am often in awe and wonder of it all. What I've realized with your help, Raubolt, is that in *this* telling, I'm not ending with the trauma but beginning there.

Raubolt's Voice

Rebecca, sometimes all we have is our story, our truth, which becomes the foundation for a brave steadiness to live beyond the expectations of others.

Getting back to the point of this chapter, "attachment, part two." Those first years of therapy were a continuous push and pull as far as my attachment to you was concerned, Raubolt. Wallin (2007) described attachment relationships for traumatized people as "overwhelmingly painful," and I would have to agree. Attaching to anyone, for me, was something I longed for, craved deeply. But, attaching also felt akin to walking around without a layer of skin. A seemingly gentle breeze of care from another, from you, felt as though I might burst into flames. I remember moments in those early sessions when I thought I might fall to pieces. Those moments weren't when I was telling you about trauma, though that could leave me wrung out and exhausted. The times when you were tender with me, when you'd offer a moment of connection, were actually the most difficult. I would want to scream, run, weep, and cling to you all at once. And, I was determined not to let you know that all of this was happening because I was sure you'd make me leave, or you'd do something sexual, or you'd tell me I was "too much."

Wallin (2007) aptly observed that the problem for traumatized patients is that they may consciously want their suffering to be relieved while unconsciously feeling compelled to recreate with the therapist the "old, profoundly unsafe relationship in which neither help nor hope" (p. 244) is possible. I wish that I could say that I was an exception to this. Looking back, I now realize how much I both hoped for a safe relationship with you in which I could heal and grow while also wanting to repeat the confusion of the relationship with Bob.

Raubolt's Voice

Rebecca, you are describing what I believe is the core of therapy. While there was all the intensity of transference, there was something else. Developing alongside these existing feelings, there was a new relationship being formed. A "real" relationship between us that would be tested and retested time and again until its existence could be counted on, even in times of turmoil and doubt.

I remember being so angry with you because I'd "fallen in love" with you, and you were not in love with me. I spent so many sessions expressing this anger to you. I threatened to end therapy because of it. I wept. I nearly begged to be loved. (Sometimes, this can still happen when I'm feeling particularly vulnerable, though the feelings usually pass much more quickly than they did then). It's uncomfortable to realize now that I was trying to relate with you the way that I'd related to all of the men in my life before you. I was trying to attach the only way I knew how to – with romance and sex. But you weren't moving toward that, neither were you moving away from me. You were staying exactly still in the relationship, close but not invasive. I didn't know what to do with that.

Raubolt's Voice

Rebecca, I surely did not always feel "exactly still." Your anger I welcomed, as you expressed both the need to be loved and the budding awareness that it could not be achieved using Bob's rules. What could unsettle me was the pain, physical and emotional, I could see as I resisted your desires for something that could not be. Yes, I could love you, but not on the terms your past would have dictated.

I didn't leave, but I didn't know how to live through it all.

Luckily, I'd settled enough into the attachment that I could count on you for the things that came next. I didn't realize that my childhood trauma was about to interrupt my adult life in a much more tangible way than through processing memories in therapy, but that is exactly what happened in our sixth year of treatment. Everything would become so chaotic and terrifying, but I'd established enough attachment that I was able to lean into my relationship with you. This is what buoyed me as the waves threatened to capsize me.

References

Wallin, D. J. (2007). *Attachment in Psychotherapy*. Guildford Press.

Wolf, E. (1995). Brief notes on using the couch. *Psychoanalytic Inquiry*, *15*(3), 314–323. https://doi.org/10.1080/07351699509534039.

Chapter 4

A Whole New Way of Reliving Trauma

By 2005, I'd begun to settle into my adult life. I'd had a baby the year before, something I'd been told wasn't likely because of multiple issues, including scarring from sexual abuse. I had been married to Jack for four years. I'd been in therapy with you, Raubolt, for about six or seven years. I worked for a Community Mental Health (CMH) center as a child and adolescent therapist. I owned a home – a modest home but larger than any place I'd ever lived before. I was coming to terms with what had happened to me and had begun to think about myself, if not "over" the trauma, as at least creating a life on the other side of it.

I'd been trying to create a tentative relationship with my mother. I felt I needed to do this if I were going to be an actualized, healthy person. In fact, a priest had told me that the only way I was going to really heal was by forgiving her (and my stepfather). I would see her every month or so, though it was very difficult.

Raubolt's Voice

Rebecca, I would like to say a few things about forgiveness. Many times, in my long work with trauma survivors, there comes a point where the fear, rage, and numbing sorrow of loss begin to fade. I have great respect for the resiliency and courage of these wise and weathered souls. They have lived through both the violence and in re-telling, often re-living, the very destructiveness they seek to heal from in therapy. This healing, this discovery of an internal, resilient sense of self beyond the attribution of victim, to whatever degree possible, is not often accomplished by forgiveness.

While forgiveness is held in high regard, we must remember it is a concept with religious implications and biblical history, and as such, speaks with declarative urgency. Unfortunately, too often, there is the moral imperative that demands one remains compromised and pathologically attached to an internal sense of victimhood without forgiveness. In this dichotomy, to forgive is good, not to forgive is bad. Such

DOI: 10.4324/9781003604723-4

a position implies judgment and negative assessment, i.e., only through forgiveness is there true resolution. This, I believe, runs dangerously close to blaming the victim and disrupts working through by running the risk of offering a shortcut and avoidance of healthy aggressiveness, autonomy, independent thought, initiative, and resiliency. It can also leave the patient vulnerable to "serial mendacity" from those who seek forgiveness only to violate and abuse more freely. Forgiveness can be too much to expect from those who have had to sacrifice their lives to the abusive proclivities of others. The options then are unforgiveness or nonforgiveness.

I distinguish the two in the following ways. Unforgiveness is about holding on to, grasping, grabbing, swallowing, biting into experiences with will and hardness. This is an active, albeit unconscious resistance; justification is infused with vengeful fantasies, memories, wishes, dreams, and often actions. Still, it remains an infected, dangling attachment to the transgressor: "I keep us alive by punishing you. Punishing you, I undo the past. I am you; my pain is your encrusted being, all of you. You will not escape. You are all I suffer and exist beyond redemption." Identification and infusion darken the soul, and mourning is sacrificed.

Unforgiveness, however, may serve us as an initial gateway, not necessarily to forgiveness, but to nonforgiveness, as I am defining it here. Akhtar (2018) wisely notes revenge can impart a sense of mastery and a loss of innocence as the victim can, perhaps for the first time, "taste the pleasure of sadism." We can go further and posit a legitimate, healthy, willful unforgiving if to forgive is to condone violence. Such a decisive action reflects a developing sense of self externally focused on such social issues as justice and accountability.

Nonforgiveness is different. It is letting go, being fed up with, moving elsewhere, beyond restraint, filling in life, redirection emerges as memories become washed out, fading into a muted background again mostly unconscious. Time has been run through in acts of psychic survival. The transgressor is crowded out, choked off by different transitional experiences (Winnicott), the vitalization of imagination and fantasy, and the gentle shiver of physical awakening. It happens quite suddenly – a "gone-ness" – or, as one patient put it to me, "a sacred emptiness." Nonforgiveness is outside the black hole, outside the teratoma, as Vida has pointed out (Personal communication June 19, 2012). Memories remain, we never forget, but they are distant, humbled, although potentially activated in some lesser form by other transgressions, trauma, or new losses. The healthy tissue cannot evade or avoid what used to be there, but what used to be there is no longer active.

Most significantly, there is no internal conversation of blame, defense, or justification in nonforgiveness. "It's gone." Often surprisingly so. The squawking shadow haunting life disappears around a mind's corner, turned many times before, but now, inexplicitly, the landscape is different.

Jack, my former husband, once described how I would "be pretty stressed out the week before she came, very stressed during the visit, and a different kind of stressed for the week after the visit." That would leave one week of relative calm before the cycle would begin again. Still, I felt that it was for the best that I let go of the past.

Several therapists had expressed to me that the most important way to heal from my trauma was to spend less time focusing on what had happened in my childhood and to instead focus on what I wanted with my life. I don't remember you ever saying anything like that, Raubolt, but by the time I got to you, I was pretty determined to create the life I had always dreamed of having. I wanted to feel secure with a family and a job and a life. And, in 2005, I was trying to let go of anger at my mother.

When I had finally had my baby after years of trying, I think I tried to convince myself that my mother was going to have an awakening of sorts. I'd believed she would self-reflect and become the mother I longed for. Looking back at how much I smoothed over in those first few months of my child's life, I realize I was trying to create a Hallmark ending to my traumatic childhood and adolescence. I told myself she wasn't really to blame for the sexual abuse in my childhood. This, despite her participation in the household-enforced nudity, making us go to nudist camps, and her ignoring times when we were physically abused by our stepfather. I also reasoned that my having to live with two different sets of unofficial foster parents, first at 15 and again at 17, because my brother was having manic episodes during which he tried to kill me was because my mother was actually trying to help me survive by kicking me out of the house. But, my mind couldn't relax into this story. Instead, my body revolted by creating the stress before, during, and after her visits.

I've witnessed my own patients do a similar re-writing of relationships and the overarching anxiety they experience when trying to remain in relationships with people who have or are currently hurting them but have not "owned" and relationally healed that harm. An internal split is created for the patient between expectations of loyalty to a parent or family member and recognition of the abuse they'd sustained at that persons' hand, leaving them feeling anxious and unmoored. Sometimes, if the person who harmed the patient takes genuine responsibility for their previous action and diligently works to repair the relationship, there can be a new relationship between them. When the person harmed is allowed to express their anger and hurt, and it is received and accepted by the perpetrator, the patient isn't burdened by the anxiety of the internal split. This was not what happened with my mother, however, and my body betrayed the anxiety I experienced whenever I interacted with her.

I wanted desperately for my child to have a different life than I'd had, and I believed that the only way I could create that was to have a good relationship with my mother. I remember telling you something to this effect, Raubolt. I remember telling you that I'd decided that I was going to forgive my mother now that I was a mother. I explained that I understood that she'd been unbelievably young when she'd had me, that she'd not known how to be a mother, really. That most of the trauma was Bob's fault. That she was a victim of circumstance, just as she'd told me several times during my childhood. The funny thing is, I don't remember you saying much in response to this declaration. I didn't feel you objected, but I don't remember believing you were in support, either.

I should explain something here about my brother. It is important to fully understand the rest of what happened. Matt began demonstrating some severe mental health issues beginning in adolescence. Really, though, he had always been emotionally explosive. As a small child, he was almost always in trouble with the adults. He would throw himself on the ground and scream; he would disobey, push all of the boundaries. He was angry almost all of the time. The fact that my mother was being physically abused while she was pregnant with him likely had some impact on his developing brain that subsequently impacted his ability to emotionally regulate.

When we were very young, I was the person who could calm my brother. People would remark on how I seemed to be the only person who understood him. In elementary school, his teachers would come to me when he was "out of control." In truth, as a small child, I loved and hated my brother. I loved him fiercely when we were very little. He was the only person who really grasped what it was like to live in our world. I wished I could marry him because I couldn't imagine my world without him there every day.

But, he was also the source of a lot of stress for me. His rage would get him into trouble, and sometimes, me along with him. I would feel so much stress when he would scream or demand or act out. It felt as though I was supposed to be able to stop him but couldn't. I experienced shame for him. I carried it around, felt its weight on my chest, while he seemed unfazed by shame's chokehold. And, I resented him for it.

When Bob left my mother, she came apart. She retreated to her room, slept when she wasn't working. I would hear her sobbing in her room. She threatened, several times, to kill herself. Sometimes, she would leave the house in the middle of the night, and I would imagine her dying someplace, leaving me to care for my brother. The house we moved to was dark and small and smelled of cigarettes. She lost so much weight, she looked skeletal.

I was 12 and Matt 11 when Bob left. As I mentioned, Matt had always been unpredictable, his moods volatile. But, when Bob left and my mother retreated into herself, Matt's mood became even more erratic, and he became physically violent. As I mentioned, he tried to kill me more than once, and this led to me having to move into other people's homes. My mother refused to get him the help he needed, telling me that all teenage boys were violent, that I was overreacting, that things would be fine if I didn't get so afraid. She encouraged me to learn martial arts so I could defend myself.

Raubolt's Voice

Rebecca, for some reason, I still find it startling that your mother was so oblivious or in so much denial about your brother that she considered self-protection to be the only way you could protect yourself from him. Embedded in that simplistic formula is a profound misunderstanding of what children, both you and your brother, needed from her in the form of parental guidance: secure safe boundaries and reasonable structure. I also believe such a stance may be indicative of a thought disorder, perhaps not in the classical or traditionally defined way, but such thinking does reflect a poor grasp of reality, delusion, deregulation of impulse control, and odd, idiosyncratic thinking. She was a danger not only to herself but to you as well. While some of these symptoms may not have been on display to many outside your home to see, they were still highly disruptive to your mother's ability to function, protect herself from predatory men, and guide her in establishing and implementing appropriate child-rearing practices.

By the time we were in our 20s, Matt had been formally diagnosed with Bipolar disorder. At first, I didn't believe the diagnosis, though I don't know why I denied it, looking back on it now. He definitely had episodes in which he would call me at all hours of the night and day, telling me of some new scheme he had for making money or changing careers. He would become violent regularly, assaulting our mother (though she would later deny it happened).

When I was about to turn 31, my former husband's mother became terminally ill, and I cared for her in our home while she died. It was a complex time, heavy with grief and the relationship dynamics of my husband's family. And, Matt began calling daily in some kind of crisis. During one of these calls, fatigued by the powerlessness I was feeling, I'd told him that I would help him get into a facility if he was willing to get some help and take some medication. I didn't really believe he would follow through, but I felt obligated, both as his sister and as a mental health clinician, to offer the help.

On my birthday, my mother-in-law died. And, moments after they'd removed her body from our house, my brother arrived, saying he needed to go to the hospital. Dazed and exhausted, Jack and I drove him to the local assessment center, where Matt proceeded to tell them he didn't really need help. Faced with the option to certify him into the hospital or let him go, we decided we didn't have the energy to fight him. He drove away from our house four hours later.

Do you remember this time, Raubolt?

Raubolt's Voice

Rebecca, yes, I remember. I was thinking, in reading your last few pages, about the role silence has played in our work together. There have been times when I have thought to say something or that you have asked me to do so in making a point, clarifying, or interpreting a remark or incident you have recalled, and I hesitated. There have been a number of reasons, but two seem the most pertinent. When you have been talking (or writing) in a way that continues to be productive, i.e., linking thoughts and experiences, discovering and exploring both the past and present in an emotionally engaged manner, or needing time to vent, protest, or assert yourself in ways not open to you as a child, I wanted to give you the space you needed. At these times, I became quietly attentive, greeting your experiences with the respect they deserved. The other significant reason propelling my silence was based on my clinical experience. Unlike some in our field, I believe telling the "trauma story" is crucial and not just when it has been a secret. There are clinicians who believe retelling the story can be re-traumatizing or can serve defensive purposes by trapping the patient in the past. While that is a risk, I don't believe it is a substantial one. From my experience, I rarely hear the same trauma story over and over. Much like the retelling of a dream, these stories change as more is revealed, understood, and worked with in therapy. If this process becomes flattened out or repetitive, then my assistance in clarifying the "stuckness" is warranted. This, as you know, can result in an interpretation, clarification, or confrontation to address resistance to going forward. The problem, in this case, may be the impatience of the clinician, not the rendering of the story.

I remember it as a bleak, gray time of my life. I was working so much then, seeing patient after patient, trying to build a life with Jack, trying to get pregnant. My mother and brother were a background vibration which occasionally crescendoed and threw me to the ground in its wake.

So, by the time I'd had my baby, I was in the habit of dismissing anything to do with my brother as an outcome of his mental health concerns. He was erratic, unpredictable, and generally destructive.

On my child's first birthday, my mother told me that my stepfather, Bob, had been arrested for the sexual abuse of my brother and me, and he was being extradited to Michigan from Florida. Typing this now, I feel some remnants of the jolting surprise I felt that day. I remember staring at her, my mouth half open, speechless. Then, my mind cleared and came to the conclusion that this must be a delusion cooked up in my brother's injured mind. I said as much to my mother, furious at her for believing the delusion began to roil in my stomach. A vague question about her participation in this delusion tugged at the back of my mind. A recognition that she would take the attention away from my child's first birthday and shift it to this history, this trauma.

She insisted that what she said was true. She said Matt had gone to the police in the city where we lived when we were children and that the police found Bob and were bringing him back to Michigan. She said Matt was sure he would get some kind of compensation for what had happened. I exclaimed that this wasn't how the law worked, that there was no such thing as compensation for what had happened, that Bob had been gone for 20 years, that the statute of limitations was past, that none of this made any sense. I think I began to scream at her. I don't remember how she left; I just remember a blank numbness shrouding me.

The next day, at the urging of Jack, my former husband, I called the police department my mother told me had arrested Bob. Jack, like me, believed it was some kind of lie or delusion, but he knew I wouldn't feel resolution until I knew for sure. When I called, I explained what my mother had told me and asked if there was any truth to what she'd said. The detective informed me that my brother had, in fact, gone to the station and filed a complaint, but "he was so erratic and confusing that we didn't know what to make of what he was saying." The detective then asked me if we had been sexually abused by our stepfather, as my brother had accused. When I confirmed that we had been, he asked that I come into the police station and file a complaint.

I didn't want to go. I didn't want anything to do with Bob or my stepbrothers or that period of my life. I had moved on, as therapists had encouraged me. I'd gone to college and grad school. I'd gotten married and bought a house and had a child. I was in therapy to address the trauma. So much therapy.

My brother wasn't doing very well, though. He struggled to maintain a job. His marriage lasted less than six months. His moods were erratic, and he still occasionally assaulted our mother (which she would deny hours after she told me he had). Somehow, however, he'd gotten himself together enough to go to the police. He apparently wanted them to do something about what had been done to us.

I drove three hours to the city where I grew up and had a meeting with the detective. Being interviewed by a detective about sexual abuse is not like being interviewed by a therapist. I remember thinking this as I was interviewed. There isn't empathy or taking your time or any right to say, "I don't really feel like I can go there today." It requires you to disclose details of what happened and when. You answer the same questions posed in every possible form. It takes hours. You have to write down your statement.

At the end of the interview, the detective said he wanted to pursue charges against my stepfather. He explained that because Bob had left the state after he left my mother, the "clock" on any charges had stopped, and while he was gone, laws had changed. Criminal Sexual Conduct in the First Degree (CSC-1) no longer has a statute of limitations in the state where I lived. The detective said he wanted to see what he could find out about Bob and what had happened to us. But, I would need to agree to press charges to be a part of the investigation. Because Matt was "too erratic" to help with the investigation, they would need me to be the main person seeking justice.

When I look back on the decision to move forward with pressing charges, there is no way I could have realized what would happen. I was stunned that the detective even wanted to pursue the case because it had been so long ago. It seemed surreal, as though I'd somehow made a wrong turn into some other reality. I wanted to tell the detective that I didn't really have time for this, that I was a new mother, that I didn't want to have to "prove" what had happened to me. But, Matt seemed to need this – it was the first time he'd really done anything to help himself deal with what happened.

I remember telling you about that interview, Raubolt. I remember staring at that ceiling in your office, terror coursing through my body, making it hard to feel anchored to the planet. I felt like I could float away, could vomit, could scream. I'd said "yes" to the detective when he wanted to know if I wanted to press charges without processing it with you. In your office, I wished I could take it back, could call the detective and offer my apologies so I could get back to my life. But, I also remember thinking I have to follow through, because to call the detective back would be akin to saying that the abuse hadn't happened or that it didn't matter. Ultimately, though, it would mean that I wasn't willing to protect my brother. And, I'd already felt like I'd failed him and that not helping now would mean I wasn't a good sister.

I think both you and I weren't sure what to make of the fact that the detective wanted to investigate. I seem to remember you suggesting that it would be okay to let it go, but your comments were tentative. It was such an unusual case. The investigation of sexual abuse from more than 20 years earlier. This was before the "Me, Too" movement. I think, looking back at this early part of the process, that we both thought it would come to nothing.

When the detective did find Bob, he was in Nevada (not Florida, as my mother had insisted). The detective told me that when asked if he'd sexually abused us, Bob had said, "Yeah, so? What about it? What are you going to do about it?" He'd apparently thought the statute of limitations was over, as well. This comment is what likely made the detective pursue the case more than anything else. I could tell when speaking to the detective on the phone after his conversation with Bob that he wanted to arrest him.

Another thing I learned about the court system is how long everything takes. Weeks pass without hearing from anyone. The detective would call, ask questions, tell me what he was doing, and then I would hear nothing for weeks. I'd ease back into my life and then suddenly I'd be pulled back into the past, having to explain again what had happened. It was like waiting for a bomb to explode or the boogey man to pop out of the closet. Except everyone expected you to go about your life in between the explosions or the horror film scene.

During these first months of the investigation, my mother would tell me all of the ways she was helping. She'd tell me of these conversations she had with the detective, how she answered all of his questions. The detective explained that my mother had refused to talk with him, wouldn't answer his calls. When I confronted her about this, she would deny it, telling me that the detective hadn't called her. So much like my childhood, these interactions began to take a toll on my mind.

I was already frayed. I was having to talk about childhood events with strangers. I was terrified that my stepfather or step brothers would show up at my door or try to steal my baby or . . . my mind was a dark forest of possible dangers brought on by my decision to move forward. So, my mother's twisting of the truth, making herself a hero, when the detectives had no reason to lie to me, was too much for me.

You said one of the most important things ever said to me during this time. You'd been trying to give me permission to stop all contact with her. Other therapists had suggested I stop talking with her. In fact, one of the conditions of my release from the psychiatric hospital was that I stop speaking to my mother "for a while because she's obviously damaging to you." But, I'd felt guilty, felt like a forgiving person would stay in a relationship with their family no matter what.

In a session shortly after my mother had again lied about her "helping the investigation," you'd said,

Your whole life, you've been trying to get through the swamp that your mother created around you. You've been able to move through it, sometimes just barely. Often, only your nose has been above the surface enough to keep you alive. Sometimes, you've needed a straw to get enough air. But, now you're carrying your baby. Do you want your baby to have to struggle to get air, too? Because she will do that around the baby, too.

Raubolt's Voice

Rebecca, reading my words after the many years that have passed creates mixed feelings for me. While I am pleased they had the desired impact, I am struck by the awkwardness of my phrasing. As you know, I seldom tell someone what they should do about any relationship, let alone such a significant figure as a mother. In this case, your mother's egregious behavior was matched only by her relentless self-serving pursuit to

dismiss reality when it conflicted with her wish to be the hero. She per-
fected the art of "gaslighting" long before the term entered current-day
parlance. She would stop at nothing to deceive you into believing that
she was on your side while systematically undermining your attempts to
seek accountability and justice. She chose to support, through lies and
obfuscations, the man who raped her daughter instead of her daughter
as a child and now as an adult. I was concerned at the time she would
prevail unless a strong counter-argument could be mounted to contain
her. I chose to highlight your desire to protect your baby to dramatize
both the history of her behavior but also the lengths to which she
would go to proclaim her "innocence" no matter the cost to others.
Recognizing this malevolent narcissism, I sought to expose and contain
it using the most powerful images I could imagine.

And, that was it. Nineteen years ago, I sent a letter ending all contact with her.
I felt like I could breathe more easily after I sent it, because I knew that I meant
what I'd written and that I wouldn't reconnect with her. This decision has caused
a lot of guilt over the years and a challenge to the idea that I was a basically kind
person. Yet, I've never regretted it, nor have I missed her in my life. I have missed
the idea of having a loving mother but not the person who was my mother.

Once the detectives completed their investigation, the case was referred to the
Prosecuting Attorney's office. I could tell you were worried about my upcoming inter-
view with the Assistant PA during the sessions leading up to my scheduled interview.
In one of those sessions, I actually thought of you for the first time as like a father.
I imagined what a daughter would feel seeing her dad worried for her and powerless
to protect her. I feel the same lump in my throat that I felt when I first had that thought.

Toward the end of the session we had just before I was to go to the interview,
you handed me this small clay car. It had been in your bookcase for years, and I'd
wondered about it. I'd imagined a young patient had made it for you. I'd actually
wished I could have made something for you to keep nearby.

Raubolt, you told me that the car had been made by your son when he was
a child, and you wanted me to take it with me to the interview. You told me to
remember your office while I was there, to remember that you were going to be in
your quiet, peace-filled office when I got back. I hesitated, shocked by the offer,
but you insisted.

This act of kindness was one of the most powerful moments in my attachment
to you. The fact that you would allow me to not only touch something so valuable as your child's creation but to insist I take it with me to a place so frightening told me that you understood that I would need to know you were with me in
some way.

Raubolt's Voice

Rebecca, I wrestled with the question, "Was there a way to express my concern and love for you without undermining the safety you experienced with me?" I decided to use the positive transferential feelings you were describing to offer something of value and meaning for your court appearances. The small clay car my son made for me years ago provided the perfect, in my mind, answer. You had noticed the car before and, I believe, even picked it up and held it a time or two. At least, that is how it plays in my memory. At a minimum, it offered continuity and a touch of familiarity in what I expected would be a hostile environment. Since it was a personal item, it felt like I was offering a piece of me for you to take with you. The choice was not accidental for other reasons as well. Symbolically, while small and obviously made by a child, it was sturdy and solid. Since it was a car, it also implied movement and could whisk you away if need be and, if only in fantasy, to provide a much-needed breather. It was also small enough to fit in your pocket so no one would know if you clutched it to regain your balance or perspective. Being important to me, you knew I expected "both of you" to return safely. I also anticipated you would initially decline my suggestion, which allowed me to insist, in a fatherly fashion, that you take the car "for your own good." This, in turn, allowed me to introduce both levity and loving concern.

That interview with the Prosecuting Attorney (PA) was traumatizing. I've rewritten that sentence about five times, trying to find a more adequate description, but honestly, traumatizing is the only (inadequate) description I could find. I'd imagined it would be difficult. I'd imagined people questioning my memories of the abuse. I'd even considered that I would be accused of attention-seeking. But that isn't what happened. It was worse.

After answering the same questions the detective had asked during that first interview, the PA asked me about my work. She wanted to know if I worked with abused children. I'd said that I did. She suddenly switched gears and asked why I hadn't reported the abuse by Bob and my stepfathers earlier. Why hadn't I gone to the police earlier? I'd explained that when I was a teenager, I'd been afraid. By the time I was an adult, I was trying to move forward, to create a good life, as so many therapists had encouraged me to do. I believed it was too late to do anything about the abuse and that my job was to not allow the abuse to define me.

The PA then sat back and asked me how I could live with myself. Confused, I spluttered some question about what she meant. She shifted forward and said,

You've been telling me that you give counseling to children and adolescents who've been abused. You know what that does to them. But, you didn't do anything to make sure your stepfather didn't keep abusing other children like your clients.

(This is from an excerpt from my journal from that time.)

I honestly don't remember my response. I believe it was something about not knowing that the statute of limitations laws had changed, that I'd been told to move on. What I do know is that even now, the sting of her accusation pierces my body and fills me with a kind of tremor and sickness. She was basically accusing me of not protecting children and thus being complicit in other children's abuse.

I'd been holding your car throughout the interview, rubbing its sides, clenching it tightly at times. The weight of it had comforted me. But, I must have lost track of what I was doing to it because the moment the PA made that statement, my hand slipped, and I broke the bumper off. My heart was pounding, and I felt like I might vomit, and I'd broken your son's creation. I believe I began to sob because the PA's assistant, who had been quietly recording our conversation, asked if the car belonged to someone important to me.

I stopped working with children after that interview. I went to the clinical director of the CMH where I was working and told her that I didn't think I could sit across from a child again and not feel like a liar and a failure. She kindly transferred me to an adult intake position and helped me apply for part-time FMLA so that I could attend therapy and court-related appointments whenever I needed to. She really was so kind to me, for which I am eternally grateful. Later, at the end of my PhD training, I was required to see some children while on my pre-doctoral internship, but the moment I graduated with my PhD, I stopped working with children entirely. I saw some teenagers for a while, but even that felt too hard.

I remember how I'd told you about what had happened, handing you the broken car, intermittently sobbing and going completely still, disassociating. I can still feel the ghost of tingling in my limbs, the way my stomach felt as though it would explode at any moment. The look of horror on your face when you heard what she'd said about my not protecting other children mirrored my own feelings, and that helped. It helped to know you didn't think that about me. It helped to sit across from you in your quiet office. It helped to see that you weren't angry with me for breaking the car – you said a little glue would fix it. It helped to know you were with me there, that someone understood just how terrible it had been to have that accusation hurtled at me.

You said, with a look of disgust and anger on your face, that you believed she asked that question with the sole purpose of finding out how I would react. She wondered whether I would crumble if pushed. You went on to say that such behavior on the part of the PA was abusive and unnecessary. I could see the anger you were biting back. I watched you from my disconnected/disassociated state, but some small part of me was grateful that you were affected, too.

Raubolt's Voice

Rebecca, still, after decades of practice, I remain disheartened that many charged with protecting children can find no better way to do so than to ridicule, cajole, and attempt to undermine the veracity of their self-reporting, as adults. The PA's approach was not only insensitive and calloused, it was also the wrong way to determine how you might testify on the stand. Attacking your character rendered you more apprehensive and uncertain about what was to come. Through her orchestrated display of righteousness, she stripped you of the very protection needed to gather yourself, think clearly, and respond effectively during legal proceedings. If she believed her words were accurate, that children needed courageous souls to help them, then her failure was even greater. I would argue that in driving you from the field of child therapy, she robbed any number of deeply traumatized children of the opportunity for knowledgeable, loving care.

You were likely correct in your assessment of why she'd made those comments. It was likely some kind of test – that's the only explanation that makes sense. And, I must have passed her test, because she decided to proceed with charging Bob. She could not charge my stepbrothers because they'd not moved out of the state, and the old statute of limitations had run out.

Her decision to proceed meant more interviews, more questions, as they tried to piece together a timeline. Months passed similarly to when the detective was investigating – weeks of not hearing from them interrupted by jolting conversations about my abuse. They tried to find other victims of his abuse. I knew of at least two others who'd told me about his doing things with them, but I didn't remember their last names and didn't know where they were 20 years later. The PA asked me to be interviewed for a newspaper article as a way of finding other victims, but I demurred because the idea horrified me.

When the PA called to tell me they were arresting Bob, I wasn't sure I could move forward. I felt sick whenever I thought about it. I imagined all of the ways that things could go wrong. I'd been having several somatic responses already, but after her call, everything got worse.

In a journal entry from a few days after she called:

Un-fucking believable! I am actually having psychosomatic responses to stress and anxiety. I cannot get a good breath and it's all in my head. And knowing it's in my head doesn't make it better. Holy shit. Is this how it feels to go crazy?

What if this pain in my chest is a pain I will carry for the rest of my life? What if I never get another good breath and have to spend every day feeling like I am on the edge of drowning? Am I having the dreaded nervous breakdown? How ironic it would happen now! When I worked so hard to overcome and did make it and did overcome only to be swallowed whole by fear. Motherfucking shit – the whole thing. The whole fucking thing is motherfucking shit! I should have turned back when the detective asked if I wanted to pursue charges against Bob. I felt like I had to. I had to help Matt. I couldn't be a coward. But look at the state I got myself into . . . everyone saying I'm brave and strong, but I CANNOT BREATHE. I dread the simplest things like doing paperwork, or cleaning the kitchen, or brushing my teeth. Everything feels so damned hard.

When Bob was arrested, he was living in Nevada. There'd been some talk of the detectives who'd investigated the case going to get him, but ultimately, it was decided that he would turn himself in. I don't know why this was decided. Looking back, I think they would have gone to get him had I done the newspaper interview, but because there wasn't publicity, they didn't want the expense. A preliminary hearing date was set for the beginning of December of 2006, and Bob's attorney had communicated that he would turn himself in the week before the hearing.

You'd decided you were going to take the day off and come to the hearing with me, Raubolt. To say I was startled by this decision would be an understatement. I remember saying something like, "I can't afford to pay for your whole day!" This makes me cringe for that younger self. Because, of course, I thought that's how it would be. I would have to pay for such kindness. You smiled at me then, shook your head, and explained that you weren't expecting that. You just knew I would need someone with me, and you were going to be there. I had no idea what to do with that. But, I can say now that, over the years, the memory of that session has been like a touchstone when I've wondered if anyone really cares about me. Knowing you would give up a day of sessions and drive across the state to sit in a courtroom with me was one of the more healing memories of my life.

Raubolt's Voice

Rebecca, I was fortunate that one of my first supervisors in graduate school taught me to go beyond the clinical hour in providing therapy. The well-being, sometimes the very lives of people we see, can hang by a single thread. I learned to extend myself, thoughtfully but with determination. My supervisor closed every letter to me for over 30 years with "In the Struggle Together." And he meant it. When the date of your hearing was set, I knew what I both wanted to and needed to do.

Some, perhaps most, therapists would consider this decision "acting out" on my part or resurrecting Freud, claiming this was "wild analysis."

What I offer in response is that extraordinary situations require extraordinary responses. The unfolding of court procedures led me to believe that you would have few, if any, allies or even friendly faces when you took the stand. In other words, I was concerned, with merit, that this would be re-traumatizing, thereby risking the progress you were making in separating from the past. I had no illusions that my role would be any more than as a witness, but it was not only me I wanted you to see. I also wanted to remind you of what I represented. I hoped and trusted you would see your future beyond what was being attested to during the trial. Yes, I suppose it was an act of kindness, but to me, it was above all else the right thing to do. The scales of justice needed some counterbalance to achieve fairness, and if I could help, why would I not?

Theoretically, my stance originates in how I define a New, Real, Transformative therapeutic relationship as extending beyond the four protective walls composing office space. I have come to believe a therapist/analyst can only offer safety and protectiveness if there is sufficient courage to take considered risks on the patient's behalf. Therapists should be prepared to use their clinical standing and resources on behalf of their complex trauma patients. Since words have served to structure a language of betrayal, dramatic, courageous, and honest action where the therapist is tested in real-time and place may be required.

Bob fled. Just before he was due to turn himself in, he went to Mexico. It took them a week before they told me. I called the PA's office as the court date neared to find out about logistics, but no one responded. I called daily, twice a day, leaving messages, asking why no one was calling me. Finally, they called and explained that he'd fled. They weren't going to extradite him. They didn't say it, but I knew it was because that was a lot of work for a 20-year-old case with limited physical evidence.

You sat with me in that next session. Both of us were stunned by the events of the past few weeks. I think I cried, though I mostly remember feeling like all of the energy that had been used to sustain me had drained out. I was exhausted. You reminded me that we would make our way back out from under this year-long trauma.

Reference

Akhtar, S. (2018). *Sources of Suffering: Fear, Greed, Guilt, Deception, Betrayal, and Revenge*. Taylor & Francis.

Chapter 5

The PhD Program Years

When the investigation of Bob began, I decided to apply to a PhD program. I'd reflected on what had helped me through the original trauma, and I'd concluded that it was going to school and learning. Before then, I'd been encouraged for years to go back to school by nearly every significant person in my life. Raubolt, I believe you'd wondered what was in my way on a couple of occasions. My former husband had definitely encouraged me several times. But, I'd been too afraid. Mostly, I was afraid of having a panic attack in a class. I was also concerned that I wasn't smart enough, wasn't from the right class of people, wasn't good enough. Wasn't enough.

But, I knew I needed something to focus on, something to work toward. So, I studied for the GRE, knowing I'd been out of school for such a long time that I would need to relearn some concepts. I took the exam the fall before Bob fled, and I did well enough – not spectacularly in math, but very well in writing. While I didn't have any real belief that I would actually be admitted, I applied to one doctoral program. Honestly, I applied because my husband basically said he didn't think I would follow through because, for so many years, I'd refused to even consider it. I wasn't going to back down from the implied dare.

Two months after Bob fled, I received a call offering me one of the nine spots in the PhD program I'd applied to. It truly surprised me. In fact, when the professor called and offered the spot, I squealed, "Really? You're not kidding, are you?" After a moment of silence, the professor asked why I should be so surprised and if he should take it as a yes that I would take the spot.

Part of the reason I didn't apply for a PhD program straight out of my undergraduate program, like so many people encouraged me to do, was because of the psychiatric hospitalization. After that experience, I was fairly certain everyone would be able to see just how damaged I was. I imagined sitting in a doctoral program having a panic attack and being asked to leave. Or, I suppose on some level I thought the faculty would see me and be able to see through to my hurt places and know that I should not be in their program. No amount of cognitive restructuring could convince me that I was wrong.

So, when I began the PhD program in the fall of 2007, I began to feel panicky. Still raw and psychologically bleeding from the investigation and

DOI: 10.4324/9781003604723-5

court-that-never-happened, I felt like I was going to be found out any minute. I'd quit my job at the CMH where I'd worked as a child therapist-then-intake-coordinator at the urging of my PhD program, which meant I lost my sense of professional identity. Returning to the role of student, I felt simultaneously diminished in the fact that I was no longer the person who made clinical decisions and was burdened with the expectations of what it meant to be a PhD student. Where I'd previously been a confident clinician – work had always been a place where I felt competent and assured – I was now a cowering learner waiting for the ax to fall. I kept waiting for someone to tell me that I needed to leave. I would nervously ramble when talking to fellow students, all of whom were a good ten years younger than I was. I was certain they all knew more than I did and was sure they thought negatively of me. I soon gained a reputation among some of the other students as having an anxiety disorder. Little did they know just how right they were – I was terrified most of the time. The Great Recession started a few months after I started my program, which meant I couldn't go back to work because there had been massive layoffs at the CMH where I'd worked, and this made me even more frightened. The stakes were higher.

I remember you trying to convince me that the faculty were just normal people. In fact, I think you tried to make comments about how poorly they dressed and how they wouldn't likely have anywhere near as much clinical experience as I had. I remember arguing with you about it, telling you that you didn't understand how I shouldn't be there. Am I remembering that correctly?

Raubolt's Voice

Rebecca, for the most part, I remember these details as you do. What I will add is that I was trying to use humor and exaggeration to influence your assessment of the instructors and yourself. Sometimes when your anxiety is high, and you have lost perspective, old vulnerabilities and self-doubts surface. Any attempt to reason or argue you out of your feelings is rarely successful. A lighter touch reduces the intensity of the panic by providing a different perspective that is actually at odds with what you fear. I have found with you that laughter reduces the pressure while also encouraging a "resilient adjustment," i.e., going against the grain by making "fun" of the fear. Such a stance entails some risk only if you feel I am demeaning or dismissive of your concerns, but I have not been convinced that this is likely. While I have been provocative, I don't believe I have been disrespectful or demeaning. I rely on our accumulated experiences where our relationship has been repeatedly tested and where we are confident "the center will hold." Besides, most academics I know do dress as if personal style was a betrayal of the profession.

Thinking about it now, I wonder at my decision to begin a PhD program nine months after Bob fled. I have this image of getting into a car that has just been in a terrible accident, bumper hanging off, scars running down each side of it, the ominous whiff of smoke coming through the vents. And, I was expecting the car to make it across country, repairs to be made as necessary along the way. Yet, I suppose that is how I'd lived my life – I just keep coaxing the car into drive, patting the dashboard. My mind being the car, my desire to live being the driver.

One important idea that kept me getting into the car and driving forward after the court-that-wasn't was the fact that I had this 3-year-old child who was counting on me. Knowing that I was a mother who needed to show up every day. Knowing that I was determined to be a different kind of parent meant I had to stay present and keep going.

I had to keep getting into that car, but did I necessarily need to drive across the metaphorical country by going into a PhD program? Perhaps it would have been smarter for me to try to just tool around town for a bit? The thing I've realized about myself over the years is that I tend to push myself harder than is always wise. I expect myself to keep moving, to keep striving, even when I am on the edge of collapse, and perhaps I've caused myself more pain than I should have. Though, I also wonder if that's also part of what has helped me. Perhaps, the fact that I don't give myself a chance to slow down and lick my metaphorical wounds is how I've kept myself from completely giving up? I don't know any other way to be. I don't know how to not strive. Like so many coping strategies, this striving is probably both a problem and something that helps.

Raubolt's Voice

Rebecca, you are identifying a dilemma here that is compounded by my own proclivity to adopt the same breathless pace. "Going slow" never had much appeal to me, which, as you can imagine, has posed challenges in my psychoanalytic practice. Frequently, the question facing me is whether a little more effort, consistency, discipline, etc., will allow me to succeed. That I am aware of this tendency in myself hopefully alerts me to times when you push and go beyond your limits. Still, there remains the question based on a shared ambivalence as to when enough is really enough, and self-care dictates a more reflective, easier pace. You have confronted me seemingly about as often as I have challenged you in this regard. And yet, perhaps in a bit of defensive posturing, I would also add you can't argue with success.

There are so many things I learned from my PhD program that weren't likely what my faculty intended me to learn. For example, I learned that many faculty members in research-heavy universities don't actually know what it is to be a clinician. How could they? They're focused on tenure and publishing and research and university politics. Yet, they're the people teaching future clinicians how to be clinicians. And this means they are providing misinformation to people who will be sitting with patients hour after hour.

Some of the misinformation given to these future clinicians has to do with the efficacy of manualized and evidence-based treatment. I believe that the explosion of these types of treatments is due to large, research-heavy universities with faculty who do the minimal amount of treatment necessary. There is often a misunderstanding of what it is to be a full-time clinician or to work with a patient with extreme trauma. I say "misunderstand" because I believe that most faculty want to be helpful and are not intending to mislead anyone. Most faculty entered the field hoping to help. But, their ivory tower skews their view of what it means to sit in a room with someone terrified by life.

In my experience, there was also a lack of understanding about the level of trauma experienced by clinicians themselves. I mentioned in an earlier chapter the conversation I had with a faculty member exclaiming about their desire to screen out students with trauma history. I was so surprised by the comment that I believe I momentarily froze. I know I later talked with you about it, Raubolt.

I remember feeling simultaneously ashamed and indignant. While my level of developmental trauma is fairly unique, most of the clinicians I met when working in CMH settings had some form of childhood trauma. I had been afraid I would get kicked out of the PhD program because I had panic attacks or that I was potentially not smart enough for this level of education. The fact that I was the child of two high school dropouts and didn't really know anyone (other than in a professional context) who had a PhD also left me wondering about whether I could make it through the program.

It hadn't occurred to me, however, that I could be screened out of the field because of my trauma history. This became a brand-new way for me to attack myself, and I remember telling you about it in multiple sessions. I would proclaim that I was too messed up by trauma to be of any use. I would ask if you thought that I shouldn't be practicing. I remember you gently disagreeing with this conclusion.

Raubolt's Voice

Rebecca, only "gently," huh? Either your memory is off, or I did a better job disguising my feelings than I realized. I recall being quite critical of those professionals who appointed themselves "keepers of the gate." What bothered me the most was the blatant contradiction and hypocrisy embedded in their position: teaching therapies to treat trauma while not believing trauma was treatable. Am I being too judgmental here? I don't believe there are limits to what can be accomplished in therapy. True, there are scars from mistreatment that remain, but can that not be said of any number of difficult maladies? In fact, my experience suggests that therapists who have a history of trauma, even severe trauma, can have a particular "been there" empathy. If they are able to use the hypervigilance they have developed by coupling it with a felt sense for the suffering endured, it has the makings for a strong therapeutic relationship. Such professionals often understand and treat trauma from the inside out. Since I have come to understand that it is the relationship that heals, to exclude therapists on the basis of what they have lived through is as cruel as it is shortsighted. Additionally, you were aware of many of the sensitive spots where you could become unduly vulnerable, thus mitigating flagrant boundary violations or unbridled countertransference reactions that might cripple the therapy you were providing.

I remember you wondering who would be performing psychotherapy if the only acceptable candidates would have no childhood trauma. I would feel frustrated with your lack of alarm at my being allowed to practice. Nonplussed, I would ask you if you maybe shouldn't tell me to stop practicing. But, I think both of us knew that it was when I was seeing patients that I actually felt the most comfortable, the least afraid.

This, by the way, is something that I have often wondered about – why do I feel the most comfortable in my own skin when I'm practicing psychotherapy? I feel as though my resilient self shows up in the therapy office. As though the uncertainty of the outside world falls away, and my mind can usually let go of my own worries and fears. For example, during the year of investigation of my stepfather, I rarely missed work or canceled sessions despite having FMLA. I would ask you if you thought I should take time off, and while you never directly answered me, I had the feeling that you knew it was better for me to continue working than for me to be outside of sessions focused on myself and the chaos of what was happening.

Raubolt's Voice

Rebecca, you are correct. Rarely do I support FMLA for the reasons you note. Working offers structure, provides meaning, and reduces shame-filled ruminations by focusing attention outside of oneself. So, my concern with FMLA is that it can enhance, not reduce, the experience of being broken with the none-too-subtle implied belief that patients need to be protected from such therapists. My 40-plus years in the field have repeatedly confirmed this latter belief is false.

I have heard of some therapists sharing some of their own trauma with their patients as a means of connection. I have never done this. I have never revealed to a patient anything about my childhood or my trauma history. I have considered publishing this book anonymously because I do not want my trauma history to be overtly present to my patients. Part of the reason that I haven't shared my trauma history is my own knowledge of how that feels. One of my early therapists made some comments about her own sexual abuse that shut me down and made me feel angry and cold inside. She was likely trying to help me feel seen and understood, but that is not what happened. I felt like I now had to quiet my own story so that she wasn't injured by it.

Raubolt's Voice

Rebecca, you have named an important limitation when considering self-disclosure. Revelations by the therapist must be for the patient. Before discussing personal history, it behooves the therapist to ask: "Who is this for, what are the intended benefits, what are the risks, and is this the right time?" I suspect the therapist you describe meant to be helpful, but she was out of step with you.

But, quite frankly, earlier in my career, I didn't reveal my own history to my patients for a much more selfish reason. I loved the break I got from my own trauma and pain when I was in sessions. During the investigation and court-that-didn't-happen, I was allowed to focus on other people when I was working. In fact, I was *required* to think about other people. I didn't have to worry about Bob or my mother or the possibility of testifying or the Prosecuting Attorney. I could lose myself in the lives of my patients for a while.

One of the greatest losses I experienced when I went back to earn my PhD was that clinical role. My program had strongly encouraged us not to work outside of the university. (I learned later that several students didn't follow this suggestion, but I was too afraid to break any rules). I was employed by the university for a very small stipend, but for the first two years, I did not work as a clinician. The only time I saw patients was when I had a clinically focused class, and then we were allowed only two to three of them. So, the respite I took in clinical work was diminished, leaving me adrift and more uncertain of myself.

I did learn some very valuable things in my PhD program. Some of the most powerful lessons I learned had to do with the impact of culture, race, racism, sexual identity, and gender identity on patients' lives, mental health, and experience of psychotherapy. I'd earned my MA in psychology just as these topics were beginning to be discussed in courses, but those discussions were surface-level. I was told to be respectful of other cultures, but I hadn't really been challenged to look at my own identity and how this could play a part in my sessions. I didn't know how to recognize how microaggressions impacted the mental health of my patients or how I might be blinded to my own privileges as a white, cis woman.

I feel very lucky to have been required to face and learn to talk about my own privilege. I remain humbled by the vulnerability of some of my faculty and fellow students as they shared about their own experiences of aggression by others toward them based on their racial and/or sexual identities. I am so grateful to be called out whenever I tried to hide behind tears. I was generously offered the chance to really listen and learn about the ways that microaggressions eat at the fabric of a person. I began to recognize the ways that trauma is different for a person who experiences rejection from society at large on a daily, hourly basis.

I remember bringing these ideas back to our sessions, and for some time, I felt there was a tension between us about this. I wondered if you, an older white guy, were going to understand what I was learning about, if you would see the importance. I now think that tension may have been partially due to the fact that I was going through a developmental shift during this time. I experienced a bit of an adolescence during my PhD studies in my relationship with you. I began questioning if you knew as much as I'd previously believed. I wanted to push back on the idea that you were all-knowing. I believed you, the adult/parent, couldn't possibly know all the "new" things I, the young person, now knew. I'm not even sure how much you were aware that I was doubting you then. I don't remember ever directly talking about it. I just remember a mild dissatisfaction with your responses, or lack of response, to my observations about race, racism, heterosexism, gender-ism.

Raubolt's Voice

Rebecca, I was aware you would take issue with me more frequently during this time period you are describing. By my recollection, I didn't address the socio-cultural concerns you were enamored with – at least not directly. Through my relative silence and neutrality, I hoped you would use the space and impetus to challenge me about what was happening in the room. I did not want to engage in political discussions with you out of concern that this would either dilute or distract us from the transferential implications that were unfolding. There were, to my mind, already present powerful feelings of an ambivalent nature about what I represented as a male. I didn't believe adding "white" or "privileged" would offer any greater depth to our discussions, and I had no interest in an intellectual debate. I do remember trying to point out ways in which you would "elevate" me at your expense. When I thought I could, I would challenge you by suggesting you were playing it safe in talking about your disappointment with others and yet "giving me a pass." Gradually, I worked to expose and magnify our differences so that you might push against me when we had disagreements. I also wanted them to be effectively charged, real, and immediate.

I also began learning about attachment during this part of my schooling. Of course, having worked with children in CMH settings, I knew that the quality of the relationship between a child and their parent impacted how they behaved, but that was the extent of my knowledge. There'd been some odd "attachment" therapies when I worked with children, including therapies that encouraged wrapping children up tightly to create attachment, but I mostly steered clear of those ideas because of concerns about the children's safety – a child died from being forced into a hold by a therapist when I was a new clinician.

I'd not heard of Bowlby. I'd had one course during my MA studies that had exposed me to a basic understanding of Winnicott, but I really had never understood how attachment impacts a person throughout their life. That people would develop attachment styles based on childhood experiences and these styles would persist into adulthood was both a revolutionary idea to me and made intuitive sense to me based on my clinical work.

I won't get too far into the theory here. I've given a brief synopsis of attachment theory in Chapter Two with your help, Raubolt. I believe every good clinician should have a working knowledge of how attachment, when wounded, leaves deep scars that impact every relationship, and I wish I'd been exposed to the theory earlier in my studies.

I began to wonder about my own attachment style, and I became a bit obsessed with trying to understand where I would be categorized. I think this may have become the new way I tried to call myself broken beyond repair in our sessions.

I'm going to take a break from this section, as I feel heavy with fatigue talking about my PhD studies. I believe that has to do with how heavy I felt emotionally during those five years. I was weighed down with dread that Bob would suddenly reappear, with trying to be a student after being a professional for 11 years, with raising a toddler while my husband traveled much of the time for his work. I remember not sleeping much during that time. I would wake up in the middle of the night sweating, terrified of some unknown thing out there waiting to get me. I also, inexplicably, gained 40 pounds over three years.

Raubolt's Voice

Rebecca, good idea, I believe, to pause and reflect on what you have just written. The events you are raising here are "weighed down" by an emotional return to childhood experiences that were terribly disruptive and where you felt unmoored. Learning about attachment theory offered you a cognitive framework to understand where you had been and where you were going. It also presented an alternative schema through which you could provide the necessary developmental experiences for your child that allowed for more secure, loving protection.

As I wrote that last paragraph, my heart fluttered and my stomach dropped. My body seems to be remembering how hard that all was, and how alone I felt most of the time. I'm not sure why I feel the need to tell you about all of the academic gains I made during my studies, as though I must prove that those five years of my life weren't wasted. But who am I proving this to? Myself? Sometimes, I wish I'd attended a more psychodynamically oriented school, one more oriented to treatment and less focused on research. But, I'd applied to one school on a dare. I'd not really believed I would go to school.

I came out of my PhD training knowing that there had been things I did not know that I did not know for the 11 years I'd practiced with my MA. The certainty of my knowledge and ability to be a good clinician prior to the MA program was gone. I realized I didn't know enough, that I would never know enough. I learned so much about research, statistical analysis, critical thinking, about brain physiology and function, about the history of psychology, about development. I grew as a supervisor, realizing what it means to meet a clinician where they are. About the impact of culture and oppression on a person's experiences of the world and psychotherapy. I learned about my identity as a psychologist and the responsibility that came with that title. But, mostly, I came away feeling less certain, not more, of how to help a patient heal from trauma.

I suppose, in some ways, I am grateful that I came out less certain, because I think it helps me reflect more, ask more questions. But, I sometimes envy that younger self who doubted less, the self who didn't know what she didn't know.

In the background of school, there was this quiet, nagging sensation that the court issue wasn't actually over. Every few months, I would wonder whether he was coming back. I became frightened that my mother or Bob or one of my stepbrothers would come and take my child. Sadly, I frightened my child with this worry, telling him not to talk to anyone who said they were a grandparent, to run away as quickly as he could. Fears of someone stealing your young child is every caring parent's terror, but for me, there was a real sense of dread.

My mother had begun to pop up sporadically in my life shortly after Bob fled. She still does this, even now. She threatens to show up at my house. She calls my office every so often. She's commented on my practice's social media feeds. While I was attending my PhD program, she began sending these odd notes. Sometimes, they'd arrive in flowery cards or cards designed for children. Inside these cards, written on pink paper with kittens on the top, she'd insert pages filled with long, rambling letters. She would proclaim she was "sorry you believe you were hurt," followed by statements that she "never knew what Bob was doing to you." Other times, the letters would be angrier, more insistent, accusing me of being unfair to her by keeping her from her only grandchild. She would evoke my faith as a weapon of guilt.

I would sit in your office, sobbing, or seething, or terrified when these strange notes would arrive. Guilty and ashamed and angry and afraid and sick with this quivering sensation throughout my body, I would ask you what you made of these letters. I would ask if you thought I was being cruel because I didn't miss her. I never missed her. You would quietly ask me if there was any desire to see her, and I would tell you that the only desire came from a fear of condemnation by others for not forgiving her. You assured me that the fact that I didn't want to be around a person who caused me pain was not an indication of a bad person. I would gratefully take your assurance, but I often wondered if I am truly a terrible person.

I began meeting with the pastor of my church around this time. You'd been clear that you didn't see my decision to distance from my mother as immoral, but I wasn't so sure it all matched from a faith perspective. You'd discussed unforgiveness and non-forgiveness with me (see Chapter 3), but I was quite concerned that I wasn't following what my faith tradition required.

I'm going to take a brief moment to discuss my experience with church and faith, not because I'm interested in convincing anyone to change their beliefs. Instead, I think this is important because my experience with church and faith has been both a perpetrator of trauma and a source of healing.

My parents weren't religious, or at least, we didn't attend a church or talk about God or any of that when I was a child. I remember Bob making statements about there being no God. My mother told us she'd been raised Lutheran but that she didn't like church. Her grandmother, my great-grandmother, was "the hell and brimstone" kind of person, according to both my mother and grandmother.

When Bob left and my mother disappeared into her despair, my brother and I were untethered. We engaged in things that I now shudder when remembering. Often left alone with little food in the house, we would sometimes steal loose change from unlocked cars in a parking lot behind our house. We would smoke the marijuana my mother grew and kept in her room (long before it was legal to possess). Each of us stayed out until all hours of the night. This was when I was seeing my teacher at his apartment. I had sex with random people. I once got into a car with a strange man who'd followed me from the library with the vague hope that he might kill me.

So, when a friend from school invited me to her strict Evangelical Christian church, I was internally desperate for some kind of structure. School was my main source of structure, and I thrived there, but no one cared whether I was doing "the right things." I needed someone to tell me that it mattered that I stopped, and who better than God?

I was "saved" and baptized (actually dunked in a large tank at the altar of the church) when I was 14 years old. I attended church twice on Sundays and once on Wednesdays. I attended Sunday school and became the captain of the Bible Quiz

Bowl team, during which we memorized books of the Bible and competed against other kids from other churches to see who remembered the most.

Being a member of that church likely saved my life. I stopped doing all the dangerous things I'd been doing and worked on "making the right choices," as the youth pastor encouraged. We were discouraged from drinking, using drugs, watching television or movies that were more explicit than something with a "G" rating (reserved for children's movies), listening to anything other than Christian music, or reading novels not written by Christian writers. This greatly sheltered me from most of what my peers were doing, and it gave me a chance to psychologically detox from the hyper-sexualization of my earlier life. I gained a community of people looking out for me. I occasionally experienced a peace when I prayed that was unlike anything I'd ever experienced before. I felt loved by a force larger than myself when that peace descended.

Raubolt's Voice

Rebecca, as I read these last words of yours, I recalled the line from a Clapton song (Motherless Child) where he sings: "I am a motherless child; I don't know right from wrong." You were provided so very little structure and, even then, it had no code for ethical or moral conduct. Violence and sexual abuse formed the outlines of your early years in your family. Arguably, even more destructive was the almost complete lack of any life-nourishing expectations. Any definitions of right or wrong were inconsistent, contradictory, or selfishly based on the narcissistic desires of your mother or, more explicitly, Bob. As a result, there were no "walls of protection," and anything could happen, usually beyond your influence. In this mad scenario, any signs of compliance with the abuse could be rewarded with attention and momentary tenderness, while any attempts at healthy self-assertion were condemned and labeled as arrogance or defiance. Your voice of protest was silenced. The church offered you a lifeline; the rules were clear and consistent, especially in hearing a firm "No" to behavior that was destructive or hurtful to you and others. These expectations, while at times excessive, still required, to quote another rock song, "a code to live by." The church also provided the opportunity for a different definition of yourself as healthy, capable, and "normal." Ultimately, though, the rigidity of rules over meaning and purpose meant their influence would be limited.

Unfortunately, after a while, that church became a shame-inducing place for me. I remember sitting in a bathroom stall at a Bible Bowl competition when

I overheard some girls talking about how "any decent boy wouldn't date a non-virgin." Sermons were often full of descriptions of how Satan was waiting to grab my soul if I didn't follow the straight and narrow. I was given so many messages about how I was failing God that I wondered how I would ever be good enough.

While I was attending this church, my brother's behaviors began to deteriorate significantly. This was when he first tried to kill me. I'd come home from school to the stereo blaring and turn down the music. Before I realized what was happening, he was on top of me with a butcher knife, screaming that no one would care if I died. No one would miss me. I'd screamed so loudly that the neighbors called the police, who talked with my mother about "getting some kind of help" for my brother. This led to my first non-formal foster home.

I'd gone to the youth pastor about what had happened and asked if it was okay to go to see a therapist. This led to a conversation with the church pastor, who explained that it wasn't a good idea to see a therapist because this was a way that Satan could enter my soul. I'd pushed back, surprising both the pastor and myself, by saying that I really needed to talk to someone about what was happening. This led to me meeting with the pastor for one-on-one sessions with the door open so the church secretary could hear what was said. I don't know if this was done to protect me or the pastor. Possibly both of us. I took from those sessions that I was a tainted person because of the sexual abuse, and that I needed to pray more for my brother.

Raubolt's Voice

Rebecca, I must admit I have never fully understood why some pastors are so frightened by psychotherapy. That Satan could enter your soul makes no sense. Putting aside the existence or non-existence of such evil, what is the particular threat that therapy poses? To be treated as you were by the pastor in question suggests not only ignorance but barely concealed aggression and disdain at your attempts to heal. He was indirectly, but forcefully, blaming you for having too little faith in God to protect you in the first place while simultaneously considering you such a danger to himself (lest you "accuse" him, as well) that he kept the door open to shame you – the ultimate dismissal. I have unfortunately seen this pattern play out many times, and each time, it has ended in disaster with religious faith in shambles.

I ended up going to therapy anyway after a while. I can't quite remember how that happened, but my general memory of the situation was that the pastor eventually gave his blessing. Possibly, he understood that my wounds were out of his league with regard to pastoral guidance. The one condition was that the therapist needed to be "a Christian." As I mentioned, my first therapist was kind and cared about me, but I wasn't able to see her for very long. Next, I remember seeing a therapist who prayed "Jesus, Jesus, Jesus" whenever I tried to talk about the sexual abuse. She told me to imagine Jesus coming into the room while I was being molested and carrying me out of the room. She told me that if I prayed hard enough, I would stop having nightmares and flashbacks. I stopped seeing her after that because I felt like I couldn't imagine that. I felt like I'd failed God again.

When I was 16, I managed to get myself kicked out of the youth Sunday School, and eventually the adult Sunday School, for asking the wrong questions and quoting parts of the Bible that contradicted what was being taught. I believe I was ready to leave that church then, but the fact that I could be "kicked out" of Sunday School left me both shaken and strangely rebellious.

I began attending a Catholic Church with my best friend when I was 17. I attended their catechism and converted during my senior year of high school. I was likely drawn to this tradition because it was so different from the Evangelical church I'd been attending. It didn't hurt that the Evangelicals had preached that the Catholics were hell bound. The formality of the rituals comforted me, and I spent the next ten years finding moments of peace. I'd also begun talking to a priest about forgiveness, as I mentioned earlier in this book. I asked how I could be expected to forgive Bob or my stepbrothers or my mother. I asked how a loving God would forgive them. He explained that forgiveness didn't mean I agreed with what happened or that I needed to be in a relationship with them, but that it was a decision to believe that everyone has sinned and everyone deserves forgiveness. That priest told me later that he decided to return to school, earned an MA in counseling, and wrote a book on forgiveness because of our meetings.

When I divorced my first husband, however, I was told by this same priest that he would not serve me communion unless I received an annulment. I know this is part of the doctrine of the Catholic church, but I experienced it as a deep rejection. It shook my faith. I kept feeling like I had failed when it came to God, that I would never be good enough.

Now, I attend what is called a "progressive" church with a heavy focus on social justice, but the impact of those previous religious experiences has created an underlying shame and wariness when it comes to the topic of God. And, there's this strange interaction with my therapy, even with you, Raubolt. Because, while I haven't believed that there's this maniacal being, Satan, waiting to get into my soul for a while now, I sometimes worry that what is good for me psychologically may be bad for me spiritually. It is good for me psychologically to stay away from my mother, and it's likely also good for me spiritually. But, what if? What if? It has haunted me.

So, as the classes of my PhD program were ending, I needed to revisit the "forgiveness" idea from a religious/spiritual place, and I knew, as a clinician myself, that there are limits to what a clinician can say regarding faith. I needed to hear "right and wrong" answers, if that makes any sense. This need led to a new conversation with a new pastor.

The conversations with this new pastor led to a deeper self-forgiveness than had ever happened in my previous encounters with the priest I'd been seeing.

I couldn't forgive myself for not forgiving my mother and stepfather. I couldn't forgive myself for not wanting to forgive them. In these conversations, not only did the pastor express that it was understandable that I couldn't forgive my stepfather and stepbrothers and mother, but that he believed it was likely not safe for me to do so. This was something that was very similar to what you'd said over the years, Raubolt, but coming from a religious professional helped in a different way. One of the most important conversations I had with him included his making comments such as, "If we believe in a God that is more than we are, maybe we can let that God worry about the forgiveness of these people. Maybe we say to ourselves, 'God knows who I am and what I can do, and God will have to fill in where I can't.'" There was no shame here, no sense of failure, but instead a trusting in the Deity to know me, accept me, and work out what I can't work out.

Raubolt's Voice

Rebecca, and to this wisdom, I can only add Amen, and, well, maybe a Hallelujah or two.

This conversation began in the middle of the third year of my doctoral program. Whether it was divine intervention or just plain luck that I met with this pastor just months before my past tore into my world again is something I've thought a lot about over the years. What I do know is that I'm so grateful to have begun to find peace on the issue of forgiveness and to gain another supportive friend when I did. I was going to need all of the help I could get.

Chapter 6

And, Again

As I've previously described, I was terrified and raw during the first year of my PhD program. The court-that-wasn't had ended nine months before I began classes. My most vivid memories of that first semester are of my body in a constant state of hypervigilance. It felt as though I was constantly waiting for my world to blow up again, waiting for Bob to show up at my door. What he would do if he showed up was unknown – the proverbial boogeyman who lurks in the closet with a nebulous, unnamed danger. I saw him everywhere, in every crowd, at the periphery in every new setting.

And, returning to school, at this level of education, reopened old self-doubts about ability and belonging. Throughout adolescence and young adulthood, I'd felt like people could see that I didn't belong among the educated, the middle class. Some of the old feelings about how I'd grown up crept back into my mind whenever I was around the other students, around the faculty. I did not want anyone to know about the severity of my abuse, and I was not going to share about the court lest someone realize I should not be in the program.

Raubolt's Voice

Rebecca, I remember you telling me you were careful about your choice of words when speaking so as to not mispronounce or choose the wrong one for a particular context. The volume and rate of speech were also areas that could generate some anxiety. Then, there was also the concern that since I came with a different history and "class" compounded by being male that I would not understand, or, more tellingly, that I would judge you because of your background. You were, to my mind, however, obviously quite intelligent but hindered by the education you received and the turmoil at home that placed survival over learning. Your story and history comprised a secret life that, until the court proceedings, only a few childhood friends and the therapists you visited knew anything about. The public nature of the court and the toll it was taking on you left you terrified of exposure, rejection, and exclusion from your educational program.

DOI: 10.4324/9781003604723-6

Strange things did happen regarding Bob during those first few years of my program. Once, in my first year, I received a call from a man identifying himself as a private detective who'd been hired by Bob. I knew I needed to end the call, but I froze. His voice was kind, and he seemed wary of Bob's intentions. He told me that he wasn't going to help Bob because his wife had been sexually assaulted, and he didn't want to help someone who would do something like that. He said he just wanted me to know. He slowly asked me questions, and before I realized what was happening, I began telling him about how I'd gone back to school and wanted to move on with my life. I told him I wasn't going to deal with the case anymore. I was too tired. He asked more intrusive questions, more details about where my brother was and if he would pursue the charges. I remembered suddenly that this man was likely not a safe person to be speaking with and ended the call.

But, as I moved into my second and third years of school, I began to relax, to find my stride. I'd secured a couple of coveted doctoral assistant positions and was doing well in my classes. I made new friends who later became lifelong friends. I now consider some of them my "framily" (friendship family). I was beginning to share snippets of my childhood experiences, carefully, with some friends, but I did not bring up the court-that-wasn't because it was too odd, too bizarre to explain to "normal" people. Ironically, we would discuss patients who had severe trauma in our supervision groups, never reacting to their stories as "too odd."

In my program, once you've completed all the required coursework, you are to present your oral presentation to demonstrate your competence in practice, followed by the program's knowledge comprehensive exams. Knowledge comps consisted of answering four questions over the course of three weeks in written form. Students are allowed five pages (with extra pages for citations) per question. The stakes were high. Passing my comps meant I could move on to my internship and dissertation. Failing comps meant I would have to reapply to take them again the next semester. This would delay the beginning of my internship by a year, my graduation by a year. And, while it sounds fairly easy to answer four questions in three weeks, it was intense. I was also still in classes, with deadlines for papers due in those classes. One of my comp questions required that I read a 400-page book and offer a summary and critical review of the main points while integrating concepts from some of the courses I took throughout my program.

I went into my comps with heightened anxiety but a general sense that I could pass. I'd formulated a plan of attack, hired a babysitter for my son, and reminded myself that I'd gotten through all of my stats classes with high marks – a feat that amazed me as I'd not had any form of math in nearly 15 years. When I opened my questions, I felt slightly nauseated. But, I calmed myself, reread them slowly, and got to work. The first day, I knew, should be used to sketch out broad answers to each question, brainstorm where to find citations, and generally build a detailed plan for the next four days. I felt strong at the end of that day.

As I sat down in one of the offices in the clinic where I was working as a graduate associate to begin working on the second day of my comps, my cell phone rang.

I remember hesitating, not wanting to interrupt my momentum. But, as the parent of a small child, I was reluctant to miss calls.

People often describe how vivid their memories are of certain events in their lives. I know that, in reality, some of the clarity becomes overlaid with other memories. Yet, I remember the sensations in my body from that day. I remember the way my stomach dropped and the hairs on my arms standing on end. I remember vaguely thinking about the fact that hair does actually stand up when a person is afraid. I remember looking at my books, the computer monitor, the comp questions. I remember the sound of blood rushing.

The call was from the detective who'd originally investigated Bob, the man I'd first met four years earlier. Before I was a doctoral student. Before I'd moved on with my life, yet again. Bob had been caught. He'd gone to the Mexican Consulate for some kind of documentation. They'd run his name and found that he was wanted for charges of Criminal Sexual Conduct. They arrested him, and he was being extradited to the U.S.

I remember explaining that I didn't think I could continue with the case. You and I had talked about it extensively, Raubolt, prior to this call. No one believed Bob would return. Both you and Jack had made several statements over the four years since he'd fled the country that he would die somewhere else, that there was likely no chance of my ever having to deal with him again. You and I were working on putting me back together, on focusing again on my life separate from the abuse of my childhood.

I had concluded that I wasn't going to participate in the prosecution even if Bob did return. The first court experience had been so difficult, so damaging and traumatic. It had helped me in some ways, but it had left painful marks on my mind – the biggest being Bob's acknowledgment to the detective that he had molested me. That acknowledgment did validate the memories I had. I'd learned about false memories in my schooling, and I had feared that I'd somehow created memories of what had happened despite the fact that I never forgot about what happened or had gaps in my memory.

I'd agreed, at the beginning of the ordeal, to help with the case against Bob because it seemed that my brother needed some kind of justice for what had happened to us. When Bob fled, I felt I'd done my part to help my brother. So, when the detective called me on that second day of my comps, I was not ready to disrupt my life again. I was not interested in doing any of it.

I don't remember if I called you, Raubolt. I remember speaking to the detective, but I don't remember much after the phone call other than the physical sensations that I was freezing and fluttery inside.

I imagine I did call you. By this time in our relationship, you had become one of the most important attachment figures of my life. I know that during the first months of the investigation of Bob, I would call your office repeatedly just to listen to your voicemail. I didn't actually leave any messages, just called to listen to your voice and remind myself that you existed. It was sometimes the only thing that helped keep me attached to my life. Once, I remember telling you about it. You told me you knew that is why I called and praised me for doing what I needed to help myself through hard times. (*Thank you, by the way, Raubolt, for not shaming me – so many clinicians would likely become upset by the repeated calls without messages. I've read in chat rooms about clinicians finding such behaviors a sign that the patient had poor boundaries.*) So, the day the detective called, I likely called you immediately.

Raubolt's Voice

Rebecca, there are a couple of responses I'd like to make here. Calling my answering machine, listening, and then hanging up did not suggest poor boundaries to me. In fact, it was the contrary that impressed me. You used the recording as an extension of me, not unlike a transitional object, to soothe yourself as you needed. It was then also an exercise in self-regulation, indicating that you were in charge of taking what you needed when you needed it. Your calls did not place demands on me to respond, nor were they intrusions in my life.

I believe that to be successful in treating trauma, the therapist must consider both the leading and trailing edge. The trailing edge is represented in repetitive problematic themes which are explored for their roots and experience in therapy. This is the traditional focus of psychoanalysis. Marian Tolpin (2022), building on Kohut's initial thoughts, recognized that there are "tendrils" for potential forward movement within pathology. These tendrils consist of healthy childhood motivations, strivings and expectations struggling to remain viable and healthy. Tolpin states tendrils have been "thwarted, stunted, or crushed" (p.167). The leading edge, by contrast, seeks self-regulation, self-restoration, and self-protection in developing vitality, agency, cohesion, and continuity. Recognizing these qualities activates what is already, what has always been there but remained unrealized. In our work together, I sought to "toggle" between the leading and trailing edges, past and future, as expressed in the present new relationship we were building. As such, I emphasized the healthy strivings that continued to exist through the most painful and darkest of times, even as they were elusive, shrouded, and battered.

Therapists who see only pathology in the trailing edge might believe your boundaries and impulse control were poor, leading them to the diagnosis of borderline. When also considering the leading edge, or attempts at growth and change, a more complete picture emerges, and the label of borderline is replaced with strivings toward independence, self-care, and a nascent inclination toward autonomy. I should also add that I may well make myself available for contact between sessions more often than most. I don't see how a rigid one-size-fits-all (i.e., only emergency calls are responded to and the therapist determines what is an emergency) adds much therapeutically. More frequently, such a stance induces suspicion, distrust, significant fears or abandonment, and shame.

The detective hadn't accepted the idea that I wouldn't help prosecute Bob. He'd told me Bob was on his way to Michigan from Mexico, that a lot of time and money and effort was being spent on getting me justice. That he believed I needed to see this through, that I wouldn't be truly okay if I stopped now.

I unraveled. I remember having to talk to my dissertation chair and committee members about what was happening. The humiliation of that, the sense that I'd failed in some way because this had all spilled into another world I'd created. I'd shared with them that I'd had trauma in my childhood, but I'd not mentioned the court as I wanted it to all be in the past, something I'd "gotten through."

I'm going to go off the road we've been traveling for a moment and talk about something that has been happening between us in the present moment, Raubolt, as we have been working on this book. It's funny, really, how annoyed I've gotten with you at points in this process.

Raubolt's Voice

Rebecca, perhaps you have been experiencing "annoyance" with me, yet I suspect anger may be more accurate. Since beginning to write this book, you have been revisiting and "re-feeling" many painful chapters in your life. It may feel like the partitions of time have dissolved, and that level of intensity can be unnerving, especially given all that you have accomplished in therapy (and life). This has, in turn, affected our relationship with questions arising as to how much transference vs. a "real relationship" exists and where, pray-tell, is this all going? So, yes, it makes sense to me that you want to "tell me off," which sounds more like anger in the form of self-assertion. In writing with you, my role has changed (I believe it has expanded, but time will tell). I am now an object and a participant in your still-developing story. My suggestion to you to write a brief description came from the recognition you were in the best position to summarize your history. And, yes, since therapy continues, I believe such an exercise would help you with perspective as well as a "proper dose challenge." I have seen this pattern before where you say "I can't" before you prove to yourself you can, so you do. The point I want to emphasize is a helpful challenge is best constructed to be just outside your reach, or so it feels. "Just beyond your reach" is purposefully designed so you have to stretch, and when you succeed, it means something to you. The congratulatory pat on the back when accomplished is yours and not mine. As you may recall just below my signature on correspondence, I quote Eleanor Roosevelt: "You must do the thing you think you cannot do."

Today, you sent me this list of things you think we should be doing regarding the book, and I wanted to tell you off. I wanted to point out all of the things I'm currently doing other than this project, like seeing multiple of my own patients, running a large group practice, trying to stay healthy through exercise and meditation, trying to communicate with my son, who is in the middle of his first big love affair, and maintaining a healthy marriage. I wanted to remind you that you're supposed to be helping me with stress, not giving me more stress, because, after all, you are still my analyst.

That last sentence made me laugh at myself. I imagine my own patients saying something like that to me when I've challenged them in some way. Because that's why I was irritated with you. You were asking me to stretch myself a bit, though I'm not sure you realized that it was a stretch.

There was one task on that list that overwhelmed me. You'd asked me to write a brief synopsis of the book to be shared with possible publishers or editors. I sat there staring at that item on your list and thought,

There's no way I can do that. There's no way I can condense this book into two paragraphs. Why can't you do it? Why does it have to be me? This book is never going anywhere because I can't complete such a monumental task. And, you, Raubolt, will think you've been investing in the wrong person and be so disappointed in me.

And, then, a few hours later, I began to craft those two paragraphs.

As I've been writing this book, one of the things I have recognized is that this is how I've dealt with most challenges in my life. My first reaction is to panic and believe I cannot do it; I cannot face it; I'm never going to make it to the other side of whatever it is. And, then, I do start moving with this sort of strange determination.

Raubolt's Voice

Rebecca, there is nothing strange about such determination. It has been forged and tempered through decades of traumatic hell. When a child can only count on herself, the impossible often becomes just the possible delayed.

As happened the first time I dealt with Bob and the court, there were these giant, dramatic moments followed by weeks or months of hearing nothing. So, after agreeing to move forward with the charges against Bob, weeks would pass without much happening. I finished my knowledge comps. I applied for and interviewed across the country for my internship placement.

You weren't happy that it all came back, Raubolt. I remember you trying to carefully steer me away from pursuing the charges, noting that I'd done my part in helping my brother. I remember you expressing concerns about how this might impact me – mirroring my own worries. At least, that's my memory of it. You may remember it differently.

Raubolt's Voice

Rebecca, my recollection is similar to your own. I recall feeling ambivalent in the Freudian sense where I experienced strong conflicting thoughts about what my role should be. I recall believing caution was indicated because to this point, you were without allies when in court. I know myself well enough to realize that when the expression "I should" shows up, I need to pay attention. I had to ask myself what I really believed was in your best interests without taking over the decision by telling you what to do. Had I done so, I would have merely transferred my "should" to you, which, while offering some support and certainty for your decision, would have also undermined your autonomy.

I initially decided to move forward with the charges against Bob because I felt like I had to. I felt like I couldn't just walk away from it. But, over those months between finding out Bob had been arrested and the evidentiary hearing, it became clear to me that seeing this to the end was as much for me as it was for my brother. When Bob fled the country, I was left wide open. I'd disclosed, to complete strangers, about what had happened, about the sexual abuse. And, Bob's cavalier response, "Yeah, so? What about it? What are you going to do about it?" had ignited something in me that had been smoldering for four years.

Raubolt's Voice

Rebecca, I believe Bob's comment unleashed your smoldering rage and made your pursuit of justice your own and not just a gift to your brother. This transition was imperative to endure the court's indignities and sever any remaining emotional connections to him. Difficult as it was, you found a way to address the abusive violence he perpetrated when you were a child but do so with the clear vision of an adult, capable, and strong woman. And, Bob did what bullies do in the face of strength opposing them: they fold. As I write these words, I am also aware of my own anger at this man. Truth be told, even though I have never had any interaction with him, I find him to be reprehensible. Aggressive feelings held by the therapist are usually denied and lead to unconscious expression. We have been trained to adhere to a simplified Winnicottean notion of a "good enough mother" by becoming an "even better than good enough therapist." In this paradigm, strongly held negative countertransference reactions can be viewed as evidence of over-identification with the patient, so we seek to offer treatment steeped in empathy and unending kindness. Accompanying this stance is the tendency to exclude aggressiveness as evidence of dangerous, unresolved conflicts on the part of the analyst rather than a considered recognition and assessment of the damage resulting from trauma.

Hearing or sensing my anger carried the risk that you would be expected to have the same feelings and level of intensity I was expressing. To introduce the feelings I had about Bob could be freeing or frightening. My personal reactions to him are so much of my "code," or worldview, that to deny them would be foolish and detrimental to therapy. My lack of authenticity would, I suspect, be readily apparent. Sometimes, feelings are messy, inconvenient, and disturbing, and even if aligned with the patient's own, can still be unsettling and disruptive. Again, I counted not only on my experience and training but also on the therapeutic relationship. These are not new feelings about myself or Bob, as I can recall having them numerous times over the years. I have sought to hold the tension by recognizing these feelings, using them to help me enter your world. Yet, also knowing they needed to be contained and titrated enough to be useful with you. I wanted to convey I was in your corner, supporting your fight without taking on it as my own. My compromise with myself was that if I were to err, I would selectively do so on the side of expression. Silence in the face of depravity would, I feared, offer legitimacy, or at least tolerance, for behavior that was cruel and dehumanizing.

I'm having such a difficult time writing this part. It feels like I'm moving through sludge, each word an effort to put on the page. I want to write about other things: the research I was doing for my dissertation. Or the fact that my son was growing into a curious and bright little person. Or, the fact that I was able to match at my first choice for internship, a difficult feat when the match rate was only 70% that year due to a shortage of placements. And. And. Anything other than to revisit this time in between, this time of waiting.

In the gathering evidence phase of this round of the court case against Bob, I had to turn over all of the journals I had that mentioned the sexual abuse. I'd kept a journal throughout high school and college. In these journals, I recorded the things that most kids in high school and college in the late 1980s/early 1990s thought about – friendships, thoughts about the future, people I had crushes on. But, I also wrote about the sexual abuse, the way my brother was suddenly aggressive and scary, the times I had to live with other people, my unofficial foster homes, because my mother refused to protect me when my brother tried to kill me. My entries moved between sappy declarations of new love and dark reflections on whether I could live with the memories of sexual abuse.

I had told friends during high school about the abuse, and one of these friends had actually written about it in her own journal. She, too, had handed over her journal to the Prosecuting Attorney. Her willingness to not only testify to her memories of my disclosure but also give them her journal from high school speaks to a generosity that humbles me.

I had to sign releases for all of the therapists I'd ever seen. One of the places I'd received psychotherapy happened to be in the very college counseling center where I was working as a doctoral student assistant. Almost all of the therapy notes had been destroyed because so many years had passed. The one place that did still have records, and the records did describe my account of sexual abuse, was the psychiatric facility where I'd been hospitalized at the age of 20. So, while it was horrific that I'd been hospitalized, they'd kept thoroughly documented records of what I'd disclosed while there.

I did not tell the Prosecutor that I was in treatment with you, Raubolt, until the very end. She didn't ask if I was currently in treatment, and I didn't want that intrusion into my relationship with you. I didn't want you to be called as a witness because I knew it would impact our relationship. It was clear that you didn't relish that idea of testifying, either.

Raubolt's Voice

Rebecca, you are quite right that I hoped I would not be called to testify. I was concerned about how it might affect therapy going forward. In court, I would not have control of the space, and the rules for engagement were adversarial by design. I would not have the time to consider and reflect on the implications of my testimony. Having testified a number of times, I understand the ground rules, and because I do, I can paradoxically become too aggressive. I know, for example, when an attempt is being made to lead me to a conclusion I have no

intention of honoring, I can become dismissive and sarcastic. Given my
feelings about Bob and the lawyers involved and my own competitiveness, I didn't want to add to the hostile environment already developed.

When the Prosecutor did ask if I had a therapist, on the day the trial was set to
begin, I told her I did not want you involved. She, in a rare moment of kindness,
reflected, "You'll need someone who wasn't here to talk about all of this with." She
made no mention of wanting you as a witness.

The evidentiary hearing was set for the winter of 2010, and I was relieved.
I thought that would mean that if it went to trial, it would likely happen before
I started my pre-doctoral internship. It wouldn't start until July 2011. I did not
want anything to impact my internship for a couple of reasons. First, internship is
an intense year, no matter where you're placed. If your dissertation isn't finished,
which was the case for me, an intern is balancing the demands placed on interns
and trying to complete the dissertation research and writing. Second, I was placed
in a conservative hospital learning about things I'd never learned about, including
neuropsychology. I had to do testing and treatment in an inpatient setting, where
I worried I might relive some of the experiences I had when I was hospitalized.
Third, and most urgently, I just wanted the whole thing to be over with. I wanted a
chance to finally focus on what I was supposed to be learning on an internship and
not have my mind distracted by the abuse I experienced in childhood. Again. I'd
spent my entire life with my mind half-absorbed by that abuse, and I just wanted to
be able to have this one last year to focus on learning.

In the months leading up to the scheduled hearing, I remember moving between
"auto-pilot," during which I didn't feel anything at all, and complete terror. I would
"forget" it was coming, and then, suddenly, I was nauseous with anxiety about testifying. I was determined to have as little of my doctoral studies interrupted, determined that my life would continue to move forward. When I was operating from
that determination, I pushed myself through everything, ignoring the emotional
blood seeping from every tear and rip from the proceedings.

My former husband, Jack, and I had a friend, also a psychologist, who was
furious with me because I "refused to talk" with her about my feelings when Bob
fled in 2007 or about what was currently happening with the court system. One
day, this friend began screaming at me when we were visiting her in Chicago. She
yelled at me for "suppressing," or "not dealing with my emotions," or "avoiding"
the emotional blood that was so obvious to her. She yelled at my former husband
for "not making her talk about things that needed to be talked about." I felt like
I was somehow failing her by not letting her help me the way she wanted to help
me, but I also knew there was no way I could open those doors right then. I knew,
instinctively, that opening the doors of my emotions would create a sinkhole on
the other side. I apologize for the mixed metaphor, but it's the best visual I can
come up with here.

When I described my friend's reactions to you, Raubolt, I remember you'd simply replied, "You're doing what you need to do to get through. There's no right way to do this."

Raubolt's Voice

Rebecca, this "friend," as I recall, was demanding and accusatory over even minor transgressions. Since she was volatile, relentless, and unforgiving of imaginary slights she experienced, I considered her psychotic and, as such, needed to be managed and avoided. At the time, however, you had mixed loyalties given her primary friendship with your husband and, more significantly, the layers of guilt and doubt sown by your mother that distorted any healthy moves toward independence via bouts of narcissistic rage. The similarities between these women coalesced, and you were at risk of emotional collapse. Since changing either was impossible, I opted to focus on the reality of the moment by highlighting the adaptive nature of your behavior and to do so in an understated manner. I did not want to further activate feelings of shame that would lead you to become more vulnerable, confused, and entrenched in another maternal psychotic process.

I'd relax then. I didn't want to "do it the wrong way," but I truly didn't know how else to get through it all other than to move forward. My former husband was traveling much of the time for his work, leaving me a single parent to a precocious 6-year-old most of the time. I was trying to finish my PhD program, write my dissertation, and get ready for an internship.

As we were waiting for the evidentiary hearing, you began asking if I had considered asking someone to come with me. Jack, my husband at the time, was going to be gone that week for a work trip that could not be missed. But, I didn't want to ask anyone else. I didn't want too many people to know just how messed up my childhood was, and I also felt like I couldn't handle being rejected if I did ask and got turned down. You persisted. I don't know if we ever discussed you trying to come this time, as you'd offered to in 2007, but I know that I felt responsible for you having taken time off back then and the hearing not happening because Bob had fled. On some level, I wondered if something else would happen and the hearing would be canceled or postponed.

I want to take a moment to talk about something I noticed happened to me in 2006 and again in 2010, when Bob was arrested and extradited. I believe I was possibly experiencing mild episodes of derealization. Everything related to the court seemed so far-fetched, so out of the ordinary, that I sometimes had the sense that this was happening to someone else, that maybe I'd walked onto the set of a poorly written made-for-tv movie. And, I thought that everyone else must think I was making it all up or was delusional. I felt outside of myself enough to think that I wouldn't believe me if I were someone else. I don't think I necessarily lost hold of reality, but I was prepared to believe it if someone told me that I was having a delusion. I remember thinking that you might not believe the court was actually happening, that you thought I must be making it all up. I was relieved when the newspaper from the town where I grew up and where the evidentiary hearing would be held ran a short article on Bob's arrest in Mexico. I had something to show you, to show anyone who might doubt this was happening to me. However, the article got a couple of details wrong, which increased my doubt about the reality of what was happening. Does this make sense to you, Raubolt? I don't know how else to describe some of the odd sensations I was having then.

Raubolt's Voice

Rebecca, I think that during this time, you did experience classic symptoms of derealization: feelings of being alienated from, or unfamiliar with, your surroundings which appear distorted, colorless, two-dimensional, or artificial, distortions in perception of time, such as recent events feeling like distant past, distortions of distance and the size and shape of objects. Frequently, derealization is accompanied by feelings of depersonalization, and that you did not experience. This is significant because you remained "in touch" with yourself so that you could continue to regulate your emotional responses and provide some measure of internal safety, even in a setting that was threatening. This, in turn, prevented a full-blown regression where, if you were detached from your physical being, you might well have been unable to distinguish past from present, resulting in a reliving rather than remembering past traumas. While these court experiences could leave you feeling shattered, adrift, and suspicious, they remained circumscribed. Despite what you were feeling about your ability to function, you continued to perform academically at a very high level. What you feared might be viewed as delusional was actually a response to the unpredictable, volatile court proceedings where your testimony was undermined, and your credibility was under intense scrutiny.

Today, in our session, I told you how, after writing about the sense of derealization, I spent the next day vibrating with that old anxiety. That's the thing about remembering all of this, asking myself to relive, in some ways, those days leading up to the evidentiary hearing, or really any of the trauma – I end up re-experiencing some of the old physical sensations. But, it's like you're reviewing this strange, scary movie that you've seen before. Except it's on fast-forward. While you know how it all turns out, you still jump at the scariest scenes.

I finally agreed to ask a friend to go with me to the evidentiary hearing after several of our sessions. I remember feeling unnecessarily badgered by you, Raubolt, on this topic. I'd done lots of things alone by this time of my life. I'd spent several holidays alone over the years, sitting in a movie theater or curled up in my bed. I'd attended meetings with the detectives and the Prosecutor alone. I'd been resistant to asking a friend to accompany me to one of the most shame-filled experiences of my life, but I could tell you were worried about me. I rarely had the sense that you were worried, so I knew I needed to take this seriously. Before I left the last session leading up to the hearing, you gave me another "touchstone" object. You handed me the bracelet you wore to every session. I protested, remembering that I'd broken your son's car when I was interviewed by the Prosecutor. But, you insisted that I take it with me.

Raubolt's Voice

Rebecca, perhaps I was heavy-handed in my approach. If so, it is likely that my protectiveness was stimulated by the unpredictability of the court process. Yes, I was sure you could handle going alone. You had proven your resilience many times. Why, I reasoned, should you have to do it yet again alone if support was available? The question I was attempting to answer was whether to "insist" on you deciding to accept my recommendation, even if it was a good one if you were reluctant or disagreed. For me, the issue is how actively involved should I be in matters that were occurring outside the treatment room. It is not my way of working to tell someone what they should do "for their own good." Yet, here I was doing something very close to that and, what's more, believed it was necessary.

I am going to add an addendum to my previous words. I was trained, and still mainly practice, to focus on what is happening in the room between myself and a patient. The relational context provides the opportunity to see and experience both the symptoms and attempted resolutions being wrestled with. It also offers the best perspective to address the many fears, hesitations, reluctances, and resistances to address trauma in its various forms. To "go outside the room" can be fraught with pitfalls, and it can lead to confusion about boundaries. There is a very real risk that the therapist can overstep and, in so doing, take on what is rightfully the patient's responsibility. And yet, on the other hand, the therapist may, on the basis of their knowledge of the patient's internal world, be able to offer counsel to mitigate "re-traumatization."

These are not easy conflicts to resolve, particularly when therapy has been ongoing, successful, and emotionally intense. I had to ask myself why I was providing such direct guidance (taking someone with you) and extending my involvement (taking my wrist bracelet to court with you). Was I "over-identifying" with you, confusing your pain with my own, wanting to be the good protective father, or perhaps the hero, who would shield you from further harm? While these were all possibilities, I felt (and thought) the risk of doing nothing was greater, and that even if I was proven wrong, we had the therapy process to "unpack" and examine the implications and consequences of my actions.

The first person I asked wasn't able to go with me to the hearing, but he suggested another friend. I didn't know the suggested friend as well as I did the first person I asked, and I felt annoyed at having to explain to this person the level of what they were about to witness. Due to logistics and how early we would need to be on the other side of the state, I stayed the night at this friend's apartment and spent that evening explaining to both the friend and their spouse the general outline of what had happened and what this hearing was about. They both listened with care. I didn't feel judged, as I'd feared.

The next morning, when we arrived at the courthouse in the city where I grew up, we were joined in the small waiting area by the friend who'd written about what I'd told her in high school about my sexual abuse in her journal. She would have to testify, as well. This fact made me sick with shame. Even now, I think about her having to do this, having to show up in a courtroom and be cross-examined because she'd written about my sexual abuse when she was a teenager, and my stomach tightens and my chest hurts. I don't know that she will ever realize how much it meant to me that she did this for me.

Testifying at the evidentiary hearing was unlike anything I'd ever done before. Working for CMH with children and teens, I'd testified before, including in one pretty terrible abuse trial, so I wasn't unfamiliar with the court system. I knew that I should only answer the questions asked and to not elaborate without being asked further questions by Bob's defense attorney. I knew that I should take my time, ask clarifying questions if I didn't know what was being asked of me, and take a breath before answering anything. I understood the "game" that is our court system, which is about who can win, not what is true. I understood, heading in, that no one cared about me as a person.

Yet, how could I not take it personally? This was about my brother and my life. About our childhoods. About us.

I remember growing cold inside. When that coldness begins, I get this buzzing in my ears, like there's this white noise between me and everything else. I have this strange sensation that begins in my chest and spreads through my limbs. I remember sitting in front of Bob, seeing him for the first time since I was twelve, and the buzzing white noise in my head, thinking that I might not make it. I remember wondering, in this disconnected place, if I was going to vomit or die. I remember knowing I wouldn't cry, though. I knew that I couldn't cry because the tears had frozen inside my tear ducts.

The defense attorney used interesting tactics when cross-examining me. He wanted to know if I was pursuing charges so I could become "a famous trauma specialist." This was such a far-out comment that I asked him what he meant. He mentioned that my dissertation was about therapists who'd experienced trauma themselves, and wasn't that why I was pursuing charges – to prove my dissertation correct. And, if my dissertation was correct, wouldn't I get a lot of press?

My dissertation, born out of a frustration with the responses of some of my faculty regarding student therapists with childhood trauma, explored the prevalence of childhood trauma among psychotherapists. Based on previous research, and my own observations, I hypothesized that psychotherapists would have a higher rate of childhood trauma than the average person but would report higher life satisfaction. I further theorized that two issues would be involved in that higher satisfaction: earned adult attachment and the use of active coping.

Nowhere in my dissertation did I disclose my own trauma. Because that's not how a dissertation is done at a Research 1 university. Because I didn't want people to know about how bad things had been for me in case they thought about me the way the faculty thought about students with severe trauma.

By the way, I don't know if you remember the results of my dissertation, Raubolt. I found there was a higher rate of childhood trauma among the clinicians who answered my survey than the national average. These clinicians did report higher life satisfaction than the average citizen. My thesis was partially correct in that they also demonstrated a more secure earned attachment than the average citizen and used more active coping strategies, but the structural path analysis that I'd proposed was not supported. So, basically, therapists do have more childhood trauma; they are more likely to have developed an earned secure attachment and are more likely to engage in active coping. And, most importantly, they did not report higher distress despite the higher levels of trauma (Klott, 2012).

So, the accusation by Bob's attorney that I was pursuing charges against Bob in order to become a famous trauma therapist shocked me. I believe I may have grunted or laughed or grunt-laughed when he asked that question. He didn't end there, however. He continued this line of questioning until it became clear that I wasn't giving him what he'd hoped for. Then, he asked about my doctoral associateship. I worked as the coordinator of the sexual health peer education program in exchange for my tuition being paid and a small stipend each semester. Because it was sexually oriented, he wondered if my pursuing Bob was actually some kind of sexual fantasy or kink. I don't remember how I answered that, but I seem to remember thinking about how creative people can be in their thinking. I may have grunted or laughed again.

The moment the defense attorney really struck through the cloud of white noise was when he asked where my mother had been during the abuse. He said, "The houses you lived in when your stepfather was living with you were maybe a little bigger than 800 square feet, right?" When I'd agreed, he went on to ask how my mother wouldn't have known about the sexual abuse if it was happening in such a small space. Flashes of memories filled my mind of my mother staring blankly ahead, not really acknowledging what was in front of her. I believe the attorney said something like, "How could she have not known?" I responded, "I don't know how she wouldn't have known."

When the evidentiary hearing was over, the judge had ruled that enough evidence was demonstrated to send the case to the district court, and a trial date was set for the week before my internship was due to begin.

When the Prosecuting Attorney met with me after the hearing, she told me that my mother had testified as a defense witness. She was Bob's witness. The Prosecutor said, "It was clear that with that woman guarding the henhouse, it's not a wonder that the fox got the eggs."

Of course, the trial wouldn't happen before my internship. It was delayed by a month and was set to begin during the first month of my internship. My internship was at a very conservative, non-touchy-feely organization with an all-male training team.

I don't know how I managed to get myself through those first few weeks of internship. I believe I engaged the same coping strategy of my childhood – I just handled whatever was right in front of me and hoped I didn't explode from the pressure. I told my training director that I had to testify in an assault hearing, trying to avoid anything too personal, until he started to "brag" about the fact that his intern was "so important to a case that she had to testify" to others on the training committee. Not wanting to have this seen as part of my career, I explained that I was the assault victim, not going into any more detail. It was clear that he didn't want to know more by the pursing of his lips and his failure to look me in the eyes when I told him.

I do not remember the drive to the courthouse on the other side of the state on the day when the trial was set to begin. I remember it was hot that day. I remember Jack, my former husband, was with me. I remember that at times, everything seemed far away, while at other times, I could feel every beat of my heart. I remember hoping they wouldn't let me through security so that I wouldn't be able to attend.

And then it was over. Bob pleaded "no contest." He'd waited until the last minute to do this, after the Prosecutor had come to see if I was ready to testify. He waited until after I'd been forced to see my mother, who'd left messages on my phone telling me that she had "really helped the prosecution by telling them about Bob" during the evidentiary hearing.

When it was time for him to plead, I was escorted into the court by a victim advocate, a lovely person who kindly attempted to distract me. There were few people present, most of them I didn't know. My brother sat on the other side of the room. I knew he was there, but I could not look at him.

When it was over – the formality of someone pleading – I remember Bob staring at me as I exited the courtroom. And, the moment I was outside of the courtroom, I released the cry I hadn't known I was holding inside of me. And then, my legs went out, and I remember sinking and falling into a chair.

I remember calling you, but I do not remember much of our conversation. It was the beginning of a new chapter in our therapy, though I didn't realize it at the time, of course. It is only now that I can look back and say that the day Bob pled was the end of an era and the beginning of a newer me.

References

Klott, R. (2012). What Psychotherapists Have to Teach Us about Childhood Developmental Trauma: The Roles of Attachment Orientation and Coping Strategy. *Dissertations*, 59. https://scholarworks.wmich.edu/dissertations/59.

Tolpin, M. (2022). Doing psychoanalysis of normal development: Forward edge. In W. Colbum (Ed.), *Progress in Self Psychology* (Vol. 18, pp. 167–189). The Analytic Press.

Chapter 7

Living with the Possibility of Goodbye and Post-Traumatic Growing

Beginning this last planned chapter has been harder than I'd thought it would be. It's actually taken me weeks before I was willing to find myself here, in front of the screen, again. I'm not exactly sure what the problem has been, Raubolt. The heaviness I felt writing about the court may be part of the weight I feel now. Or, it could be the questions I have about whether this book will resonate with clinicians have finally caught up with me, dragging my mind and slowing my pace. What if I were to write all of this down, and we have taken the risk of letting others into our sessions, only to find that the clinicians out there are not interested in it? Then there is the question of why I'm writing this book. Is this some form of narcissism, exhibitionism, or some need for attention?

Perhaps the stalling is partially about wanting there to be a nice wrap-up of my story but knowing that, while many things did resolve or improve, some things remain difficult for me. I am not neatly wrapped up, nor am I perfectly self-aware and at peace with myself and the world . . . of course, who can be at peace with the world as it is? But, perhaps I'm trying to say too many things at once and need to just take it one step at a time, as I have done in previous chapters and have done on the journey that I'm writing about.

When the entire court experience began, I didn't believe I needed to have Bob arrested. I didn't see any benefit in having to be a part of the public experience of a trial. I never believed that seeing Bob face charges would in any way change my internal life or heal any part of my psyche. In fact, I was fairly certain that it would be just one more psychological wound to sew up with only the hope that it wouldn't become infected. I could not see anything about the court process as important to my journey.

Throughout most of the ordeal, all I wished for was that I'd never agreed to help with the case. It had been so difficult. The waiting, the fear of and then seeing Bob again, the interviews with the detectives and the Prosecutor, all ate into me. It scraped at my bones and tore away any sense of peace and well-being I'd been able to create for myself. I was emotionally ripped open and bleeding so much of the time during the court process. I simply wished to return to before-the-court, before the day my mother told me that Bob had been arrested.

DOI: 10.4324/9781003604723-7

Looking back, though, I now understand that the court changed everything. No part of my life was left unchanged by the experience. Including, and perhaps especially, our relationship, Raubolt. Just before my mother made her false proclamation that Bob had been arrested in Florida, starting an avalanche of events, I wasn't sure I could remain in therapy with you.

As I mentioned earlier, I was struggling with the pain of loving you and not knowing how to deal with those feelings in a way that was different from what I'd seen in my childhood. That pain was excruciating, and I was teetering on the edge of leaving treatment. I wasn't sure I could tolerate the humiliation I felt for loving you and believing that if you didn't do the things men had always done – sexualizing me – you must not care about me.

Raubolt's Voice

Rebecca, when we first met, I came to learn rather quickly that you had not been loved. You had been told you were loved, but there was always a part of you protesting: Why does "love" hurt so much? This doesn't feel right, but sometimes it feels good – what is happening? And most significantly and silently, "How can I survive this? How can I be different from any of you?" And, yet, you were only age 5 when Bob began his grooming with lipstick and a purse. With seductive charm, aided by your mother's silent complicity, Bob dragged you through the looking glass and into a mad world of adult depravity. That he complimented you on your looks, praised you for your intelligence, and expected more achievement than you dared to consider for yourself added confusion and ambivalent longing for what was to become your search for love, especially male love. Still, you were conditioned to believe love was sex, and if sex hurt, it didn't matter because, tragically, you came to know you didn't matter. I responded to you differently; my love was not physical, violent, or possessive. I was tender with my words and respectful of your need to "push and pull" me – sometimes closer, sometimes further away. I would fail you at times by being too impatient, too quiet, or too intellectual, for example, but you came to know I would keep showing up. You counted on me to do so, and to believe I would take care of myself without hurting you. Most disconcerting during these months was the knowledge gained through experience that I did not need anything from you, and that realization changed everything.

Would I have quit my treatment with you had the court not happened? I honestly don't know. I'd like to say I would have stayed and tried, but I remember the shame of those feelings of love for you, and I wonder if I could have been resilient enough to endure the pain and longing. In some ways, the investigation and subsequent court procedures made all of that seem much less important. Not that I didn't have sessions with you during which I felt that level of humiliation and shame about my feelings for you. I struggled in our relationship throughout those court years, but my need for a steady, caring parental figure outweighed my fear. So, I stayed in treatment, and our work deepened and took hold.

I remember once, sometime in the middle of those court years, telling you about a dream I'd had. I was reluctant to share it, but it had been so vivid and the feelings when I woke up were so powerful that I knew I had to share it. I dreamed that I was visiting your house. Your wife had kindly greeted me and led me to the couch where I'd normally had my sessions with you. She left to get me some water, and you'd called out that you would be with me in a few moments. Suddenly, when left alone, I lost control of my bowels and shat all over your couch. Mortified, I tried burying it under some of the couch cushions but couldn't cover all of my shit. I stood, intending to rush from the house, just as you entered the room. That was when I woke up.

I remember feeling so mortified when telling you about the dream, embarrassed as though my excrement was actually in the room with us. You didn't seem bothered, though. You simply said something like, "You've been having to dump a lot of shit and seem worried that I don't want to see it." Correct me if I remember that differently than you do.

Raubolt's Voice

Rebecca, you are probably right in your recollection. To be sure, it was not my most eloquent interpretation, but what it lacked in grace, it made up for in accuracy. As I recall, it also brought a well-deserved laugh or two.

I remember that as an example of the fact that during those court years, I'd decided to tell you all of the embarrassing, shameful, angry thoughts and feelings I was having, including a dream about shit.

The thing I realize with the clarity of hindsight is I had gone through some huge developmental shifts as a result of the court years. I'd faced terrifying things by allowing myself to be interviewed by the detectives, by applying to a doctoral program, and actually going forward when I was admitted. I'd lived with the fears that Bob, or his sons, or my mother would take retribution on me by stealing my child or hurting him in some way because I'd agreed to proceed with the case.

I'd gone through a type of adolescence in our relationship, Raubolt. I'd expressed anger at you, accused you of being out of touch because of what I was learning in school. I'd told you off a couple of times and lived through the fear that you would stop treating me. I'd learned that I could be angry in a relationship and not be physically hurt, not be threatened, and not be abandoned.

Raubolt's Voice

Rebecca, you never learn these critical life lessons unless there are inescapable challenges faced. We only know the true extent of our resiliency when we are pushed beyond what feels like our limits. I believe we can only know another's character by observing them when they don't know what to do and yet must do something. You didn't want to, but you carried the burden of this case – you literally went one-on-one with Bob and roundly kicked his ass. This change freed you up to express more disappointment and frustration on the "negative side" and more hope and longing on the positive side. For the book (record), I was never tempted, nor did I even consider ending your therapy because of something you said, or failed to say, about me.

And, nine months after Bob was sent to prison, I successfully defended my dissertation. The day I defended, my dissertation chairperson called me and asked how I was doing. Laughing, I told him I felt good and thought the process was going to be "really fun." There was silence on the other side before he said, in a stern voice, "Dissertations are not fun. This is a very serious thing." I said that I knew this but that "I just faced the man who abused me and helped get him convicted. This is not even half as scary." And, it hadn't been scary. It had been challenging, and interesting, and fun.

Knowing that I was believed by the police and Prosecutor enough to pursue a case that was over 20 years old had helped calm something inside of me that I hadn't known was shaking. It mattered that I was believed. The thing that bothered me for years before the court was that I had told lots of people about the sexual abuse when I was a teenager. I told school personnel, therapists, and friends. I even talked to my mother about it, who initially admitted to knowing "something" was happening but later denied that she made this statement or had any knowledge about it. Nothing had happened in the telling. It didn't relieve me or make me feel understood or lift the sense of shame – I walked around as it clung to my being. While no one other than my mother questioned whether it had happened, no one but my mother could do anything about it other than help me move on.

Throughout my adolescence and young adulthood, I felt so powerless about what had happened. I remember feeling a quiet fury about having to live with the memories, with the flashbacks, with the sense of shame. Once, during a particularly painful period when I was about 16, I'd tracked down Bob. Back then, you could call information and ask for someone's phone number if you had a general sense of where they lived. I'd known that he had moved to Florida when he left my mother, so I'd called there and was given his number.

When he answered the phone, I'd identified myself. I was surprised by how calm my voice had come out because my heart throbbed in my throat. I was amazed I could make any sounds at all. Bob's response took my breath away. He said he was wondering when I would call him, that he'd been waiting for my call. I was surprised by how friendly his voice was, how familiar, and for a moment, I'd wondered what I should say. I wondered if I'd made too much out of what had happened. But, I needed to understand. I needed some kind of release from the rage and fear and terrible pain. All that would come out of my mouth, though, was, "You molested me."

I'd just learned the word for what happened, and it seemed so inconsequential. There wasn't a big enough word, really, for what had happened in my house. So, I'd said the word I knew, "molested," and waited for him to explain or acknowledge or deny. Instead, the line went dead. I called back and got no answer. When I called the following week, still hoping for some kind of conversation, I received a recording that the phone number was no longer in service. Information told me that Bob's line was now private.

Bob going to prison seemed to unfurl something inside of me. I remember those first couple of years after the court as a flurry of change and growth for me. I grew as a mother and as a wife. I could suddenly refocus much of my energy on creating a life for my child different from the one I'd had. I knew I would need to work hard when it came to being a good enough parent. I had no real model for a healthy family life other than what I'd watched on television or read in books. I read parenting books, watched friends I admired interact with their children. I began to let myself laugh more with my child, to play more. I was still vigilant that my mother would show up and interact with my child, but it was a quieter fear. I knew I was strong enough to keep her away from my son, that I would fight to keep him safe.

Raubolt's Voice

Rebecca, you grew up during these months of court. Facing challenge after challenge, including lawyerly attempts to confuse, ridicule, and dismiss your experiences, left you cautious, but the terror of returning to those earlier years was seldom mentioned. I am suggesting that you developed the capacity to hold conflicting feelings together at the same time while giving yourself the space to actively sort through these very same feelings. As you know, the technical term for this process is mentalization – the skill of reflecting upon and understanding one's own mind and feelings. Fonagy et al., best known for his research in this area, offered a pithy summary of mentalization as "having one's mind in mind" (2018). Joseph Joubert (2006), whose writing I adore, brings to life the type of thinking/reflecting inherent in mentalizing that culminates in being able to regulate emotional states and be effective interpersonally. Joubert writes:

> What a torture to talk to filled heads, that allow nothing from the outside to enter them! A good mind, in order to enjoy itself and allow itself to enjoy others, always keeps itself larger than its own thoughts. And in order to do this, these thoughts must have pliant form, must be easily folded and unfolded, so that they are capable, finally, of maintaining a natural flexibility.
>
> (p. 123)

I began to take more chances with my career, as well. It began with me leaving a "for sure" position at the large mental health provider where I'd done my internship. A year later, I started my own private practice despite feeling fairly certain I would be bankrupted within six months. I eventually became a co-owner of a group practice, a decision I still wonder at. It has stretched my confidence and taught me about parts of myself I'd not known existed. I've had to face my fears of confrontation and learn to make decisions that others do not like. I've had to tolerate the idea that important colleagues may not like me or forgive me when I make decisions they don't like.

I, again, wanted to grow more as a clinician. My doctoral program did little for me in the way of strengthening my clinical skills, and I knew I wanted to learn how to work with my patients' attachment wounds. In order to do this learning, however, I had to face some of my own attachment trauma, both psychologically and practically.

By saying I had to "practically" deal with my attachment wounds, I mean that I had to face going to week-long trainings away from my home without my family. Because, while my former husband usually tried to attend trainings with me, he could not always do that – we had a child to raise, and my former husband had his own work to do. Attending a week-long training may sound like an easy, even enjoyable, decision. But, for me, being alone for a night can be terrifying. Entering a hotel room, knowing that no one would be around, could make my heart pound and everything would feel unreal to me. Being alone for a week could cause a type of pain I cannot explain.

Before any of these week-long trainings, I would imagine that "this time" I would like being alone. I imagined relaxing without the demands of my child or my practice. The minute I was alone, though, I would experience crippling anxiety. I experienced this sense that no one truly knew I existed, that I'd disappeared from the minds of every other person. Within a day or two, I would feel like I needed to die. Once, when in San Francisco at a conference you were also attending, Raubolt, I became so despondent that I had to lay on the floor in my hotel room because I had the impulse to throw myself from my fourth-floor balcony. I'd called my friend, who encouraged me to call you. When I did, and we talked, everything cleared, and I was okay again. When that clearing happens, it's as though I had been stuck in the middle of a fun house with all of the distorted mirrors and I'd finally been freed and I could see everything was normal and okay.

I know that I come by the sense that I disappear for others honestly (to use a colloquialism). My father disappeared and reappeared in my life whenever it suited him. One of the most powerful memories I have of him happened when I was seven. He'd picked my brother and me up for a night so we could meet his most recent girlfriend. They took us to a fair in an area I was unfamiliar with. My brother and I must have fallen asleep on the way back to their apartment because the next thing I remembered was waking up as sunlight streamed into the backseat of his girlfriend's car where we had been sleeping. My father and his girlfriend weren't there. My brother and I were in the parking lot of an apartment complex with several identical buildings. I tried to find which apartment they were in by reading the names listed next to buzzers. When I couldn't find his name (the apartment was in his girlfriend's name), I finally pressed the number I thought I remembered from the night before. A young man answered. When it was clear I hadn't meant to ring his apartment, he asked who we were looking for. He allowed me to use his phone to call our mother and remarked that we'd been lucky he wasn't a different kind of person.

My mother also had her ways of disappearing, though they were usually less obvious. She would disappear into herself, staring blankly ahead, seeming not to see anything around her. After Bob left, she disappeared into her room for a while. Then, when she began to date again, she would stay out all night. A couple of times, she was gone for so long I started calling around to the hospitals and police stations, certain she'd died.

Our work has focused on my attachment wounds in one way or another since the court experience ended, Raubolt, not to mention the work we were doing prior to the court. I'd stopped having active flashbacks, had stopped fearing that one of them would show back up in my life, with the exception of my mother, which I will address in a moment. Instead of having the very active symptoms of post-traumatic stress disorder that had been the focus of our treatment earlier in our relationship, we were (and still do to this day) addressing the impact of the trauma on my general personality. I do not say this because I have a personality disorder – something I was convinced I did have for years. I say this because childhood trauma "forms and deforms" the personhood of the abused, as Judith Herman (1997) describes.

It's hard to begin this section, Raubolt. I know you've been dreading it to some extent, as well. I find myself circling and circling this without committing anything to the narrative. There's no smooth way to transition into this part that I can think of, so I suppose I will just say it. In 2014, you had a stroke. I showed up at your house for our normally scheduled appointment, but no one answered the door. This was very unusual, to say the least. You'd rarely canceled an appointment in all of the years we'd been seeing each other. In fact, I think the only unexpected cancellation had happened some ten years earlier when you'd had pneumonia and your wife didn't have contact information to let me know you wouldn't be in.

When no one answered the door that day, I was irritated. I now know that my first reaction to being hurt is in the anger category – ranging from irritation to rage. It's a common enough response in our world of anger, but it took me some time to understand that about myself. Anyway, I was irritated when no one answered the door. I imagined you'd forgotten all about me – I'd been replaced by something more interesting. I called and left a message, likely somewhat sharp in tone, though I honestly don't remember.

When no one called me back that evening or the following day, I began to panic. I knew something was very wrong, but I had no way of finding out. I believe I called a few more times, leaving increasingly concerned messages. Then, I did something I am not exactly proud of – the thing I'd done when my mother would disappear. I called the hospitals and asked to be connected to your room. On my first try, I was told to hold before being connected to your room. I hung up before anyone could pick up. I had my answer. You were in the hospital. But, I didn't know why or how serious it all was. A few days later – maybe one or two – I received a call from your son saying you were unavailable and someone would call me at a later time. I asked him, "What is wrong? Please tell me what is wrong." Your son was quiet for a moment before repeating that someone would call me later. I could hear the fatigue in his voice and knew he was doing the best he could. I don't remember how I ended the call, but I know I realized I was asking too much of him.

The thing that was so difficult to explain to anyone at that time was how alone I felt in my fears. Telling people that you're scared and grieving because your therapist is sick does not communicate what I was going through enough. You are the closest thing I have to a parent, but most people do not grasp this concept. Even other therapists. Someone else you were seeing at the time, who knew I was also seeing you, called me to talk about the fact that you had disappeared. She expressed worry for you and then quickly moved on to other topics without much apparent emotional distress. I remember thinking that she wanted to talk about the meal selection while my Titanic was sinking.

When you called me, when you were well enough to call me, I confessed to the hospital call. Looking back on this, I realize how selfish it had been of me to make that confession just then to you. Because I believe it caused some stress, and you certainly didn't need any stress just then.

One thing we never talked about, Raubolt, is the fact that I heard from the other person who was seeing you (the woman I referenced earlier) about the day of your stroke. You'd not volunteered that information to me, but she seemed to have heard from you what had happened. At the time, it stung to feel like this other person would know more about you than I did. Now, I realize it was likely more about what you were able to share and when.

This other patient told me that your first appointment of the day you had your stroke had saved your life. Apparently, she'd realized you were acting in an uncharacteristic manner, "angry and belligerent" was how it was described to me. Knowing you weren't normally that way, she insisted on getting you help. Sometimes, I wonder if I would have realized that the issue wasn't me if you'd acted that way.

I would now, where I am in my treatment, but would I have understood something was wrong back then? Because in my history, people who were "normally fine" could become abusive and belligerent out of nowhere. Would I have walked away that day feeling wounded and not realized you were having a medical emergency?

Raubolt's Voice

Rebecca, ah yes, the stroke. I knew of your intention to write about this, and I agree it precipitated a crisis of a different sort in our relationship. Even as I type out my response to you, I remain unclear about how much to disclose, but I need to add some details that I consider significant. First, the stroke was surprising even to the many medical people involved. There were none of the usual culprits that commonly lead to a stroke. I was in good physical shape, and stress in my life was relatively low. In fact, I had just returned from being honored in Portugal for my work on trauma. So, my life was without major obstacles, emotional or physical, affecting me. The only "symptom" I was experiencing was fatigue, which I wrote off as a reaction to travel. I believe these details are worth mentioning both to provide context and to correct some misinformation.

I don't want to become defensive about details, but I doubt that the story you were told about the events surrounding the stroke came from me. I say this with some confidence because what was described to you did not occur. I will challenge only a few details to make my point; there were two men (back-to-back appointments) who came to my assistance (not a woman), and I was not belligerent. I was unconscious, so the E-unit was called.

I think there are certainly times when acquaintances or friends who are seeing the same therapist can develop competitiveness over who is the "favorite" or who knows the therapist the best. I don't know what happened here, but this line of reasoning would offer a possible explanation for why you were told what you were told.

While in the hospital, I was not allowed to make any calls, and once at home, my family hid my laptop and phone. They were rightfully concerned I would not take the time necessary to recover. I was concerned that you had probably come to your appointment only to find I was not around and that I left no explanation. I realize, as well, that this event has colored our interactions in a number of conscious and unconscious ways. I will stop here for the moment as I suspect what I have just written may contain quite a lot to digest.

Um, yes, indeed, Raubolt. Your response is quite a bit for me to digest. Today, in our session, you told me about the discrepancy between what I was told happened and what actually happened to you that day, and my mind had such a difficult time rearranging the narrative. It initially made me question whether I was remembering what the other patient told me incorrectly. I believed I was accurately remembering what your other patient told me, but what if I was wrong all of this time? So after our session, when I got home, I asked a close friend what he remembered about what I'd told him back in 2014, and he said he remembered that I'd been told the story about you becoming belligerent and a female patient helping you. How very odd to find out that this isn't what happened to you and to reflect on how that untrue story impacted me for all of these years.

The story of the hero patient helping a belligerent, ill you told to me by another patient had layers of impact for me. First, the idea that you would share so much more of your experience with this other patient but not with me had really hurt me back then. I didn't bring it up at the time, or since then, because I felt ashamed of my jealousy. It embarrassed me that you'd just had a stroke, and I was upset that you might like someone else more than me. How childish of me, I thought.

Second, the idea of you becoming belligerent was frightening to me. For some time after your stroke, I worried that you might become erratic or verbally aggressive. I'd also wondered how the EMTs would have gotten you to go to the hospital. Would you have had to be restrained? Also, I'd begun to watch you more closely, to worry I would miss some important, unusual clue that you might need help.

Third, I believe it was at this time that I'd started to become very aware of your other patients and to feel threatened by their presence in your life – particularly the patient who had told me about what had supposedly happened on that day. She'd made other comments about your sessions and your relationship before then, which had bothered me, but this particular story had left me really hurting. At the same time, I was afraid of losing you altogether because of your stroke. I don't believe I had worried as much about you seeing other people before then, but after that, I became somewhat obsessed about whether you like all of your other patients more than you like me – if maybe I wasn't as important to you as I'd previously felt.

How very strange it is to sit with the change of narrative about that event.

Raubolt's Voice

Rebecca, when we first talked about this writing project, we considered the possibility that doing so might have an effect on on-going therapy in unanticipated ways. Perhaps with more foresight, we might have added that some of these effects might be shocking or at least mysterious. Well, we certainly seem to now be witnessing a new and distinctly different narrative emerge. I knew addressing the complications my stroke created would bring me into the writing of this book in a much more personal way. Up to now, I have written about my personal reactions from a professional standpoint, meaning how either I was affected by or affected by the treatment in discussing specific clinical questions or situations. We are now looking at how a personal health issue has silently influenced therapy that, until a few days ago, neither of us was aware of. The implications that have arisen since the disclosure of this "false narrative" about my stroke are upon us. I do believe one effect that has emerged is how the story you were told increased your awareness of, and sensitivity to, my relationships with other patients. This aspect was further influenced by the unsettling description of me as "belligerent," which in turn raised questions if I was who I appeared to be or just like other men who had been in your life. Perhaps, I was more successful at managing my anger, which was one possibility, and yet another was more likely, with that being that I was more skilled in the art of manipulation. These are issues that we are beginning to sort through now nine years on. These concerns rest on top of the fears you have about my age, in general, and health, in particular. You did, after all, see me in a weakened state where I was frail and my words hesitant. This experience alone disturbed the transference, both propelling you away from me out of protection from loss and yet ambivalently toward me to keep a close eye for any sign I might not be strong enough to handle your feelings, particularly rage. So, here we are, sorting an unknown past within a known past and for a future to be determined.

The fact of your stroke shook me. It created an awareness of what it will be like when you do die that hadn't been there before. I had to begin to face the fact that a day will come when you won't be a part of my life, and I did not know what to do with that truth. Because, by then, you'd become a tether to the planet for me.

I know that my attachment to you is different from that of most patients to their clinicians. While many patients do attach deeply to their analysts, my aloneness in the world has created a different dynamic for me. At least, it seems that way from here. I know that many of my patients are very attached to me, that they would be quite upset if I were to suddenly die or disappear. There are only one or two of them, however, that I believe would feel the level of devastation that I experienced during those weeks after your stroke.

I say this not to get caught in the comparison game of who feels the most hurt, but instead, I am attempting to talk about what can happen when clinicians are treating people with my level of childhood trauma. I've noticed that some clinicians feel somewhat overwhelmed by the needs of people like me. They described feeling suffocated or will make comments about patients becoming "too dependent." What I wish these clinicians would know is that it is okay to set realistic boundaries for yourself and to also remember that sometimes your presence and care are the most healing things you have to offer. It isn't that you have to give more; it's that you just have to sit still and let the other person know you're there.

Conversely, I've also noticed that some clinicians can become intoxicated by the power they have on the lives of people they treat who are in so much pain. I'm fairly certain this is part of what happens when clinicians have sex with their patients. The sense of power and importance the clinician feels when treating someone who is as vulnerable as I have been may fill some of the clinician's own hurts, and they psychologically justify their acts which only wound their patient.

I recently met an older psychotherapist at a party who told me how he'd married one of his patients years earlier. He told me that his wife/patient had been psychotic when he was treating her but had miraculously stopped being psychotic when he married her. He went on to say that she'd "sadly relapsed since then" but did not connect how he may have harmed her by mistaking her admiration and need for romantic love. I remembered something an old professor once said to our class, "You aren't as smart or wonderful or perfect as your patients think you are. Don't get so sucked in by your own needs that you can't see what your patient actually needs."

Back to the idea that I was impacted by your stroke – that it terrified me, really – and what I want clinicians to know about treating people with severe trauma. I suppose what I want to say to clinicians about this is that your patients with this level of trauma are going to attach differently than patients with other types of concerns. What I want to say to you, Raubolt, is that I'm grateful that you don't seem upset or put off by my connection to you, and you also don't use that power to hurt me.

When you returned after your stroke and heard how scared I was, you didn't shame me. You instead told me that you and your family talked about how to handle such events in the future so that things might be communicated better. I have no idea whether that's what happened with your family, but the fact that you felt it was important to consider felt somehow helpful. I didn't feel ashamed or embarrassed at having such a need. In fact, it seemed like you thought it was a normal need. How healing is was to hear that my needs were normal and made sense.

It took some time to trust that you were actually okay after your stroke.

Raubolt's Voice

Rebecca, this, to me, is an ongoing concern. Even as the memory of the stroke fades, you have seen and experienced me as more vulnerable than anticipated, so much so that there is a co-mingling of the real and imagined. Saying "goodbye" was never going to be easy, but the stroke seemed to speed up and intensify discussions about ending therapy before necessary. Perhaps, too, this represents an additional competing emotional necessity also in play. This necessity, of course, being an ending carried out before the choice is taken from you. What I am suggesting here is that my stroke disrupted and confused the natural mourning process, so much a part of intensive, long-term analytic work. Before considering how you might conclude your therapy, under what conditions you would feel "enough had been done," there needed to be a "me" to end with. The stroke introduced the possibility of a very real, actual, and permanent loss – death. We are unpacking the implications of this possibility even as we continue to write about the process.

During that first session after the stroke, you were so pale and fragile-looking. You'd always looked strong and healthy before then, and it took my breath away seeing you so vulnerable. I felt nervous whenever you were even a second delayed in answering the door. I remember telling you later that I'd wished I would have hugged you that first day back. I kept trying to prepare for loss but eventually realized I would never really be prepared to say goodbye.

And, as happens after every dramatic event, time passed and things settled down into a new normal. You seemed to get stronger every session, and I found myself relaxing. I remembered other people I knew who'd had strokes and were okay. You'd made some jokes about the stroke only impacting your ability to do math, which wasn't needed in doing analysis. I didn't really want to think about you dying, and I didn't want to process my fears in our sessions. I remember times you'd ask me about how I was feeling about the stroke, and I believe I would offer half answers. It wasn't that I was avoiding it. I didn't know how to talk about it more than I did.

Instead, I remember trying again to figure out how to handle the relationship with my mother. She had begun to stalk me. There really isn't a better way to explain what she was doing. She called my office and left strange messages that were picked up by my support staff. She sent letters threatening to show up at my house. I began to return her letters unopened. I sent a letter telling her that while I did forgive her and wished her well in her life, I needed to stop hearing from her. I tried to explain that when she was in my life, I only felt rage. I tried to explain that it was easier for me to love her if I didn't have to continue to be hurt by her in the present.

My mother once mailed me a strange evaluation of me that her therapist wrote despite the fact that I'd never met the man. In this odd assessment, he made strong recommendations that I reunite with her and have family therapy with him. I don't remember what he diagnosed me with, but I remember that I didn't look good in this report. I remember becoming so upset that I was screaming when I called you. You'd been as flummoxed when you read the report as I had been. I remember feeling relieved when you told me that the man was, in essence, "a quack." I gave you permission to make contact with him, and you told me that you'd called and told him that he needed to "stop interrupting" your treatment of me. I remain so grateful for your willingness to intercede on my behalf on that issue.

Raubolt's Voice

Rebecca, actually, I was more aggressive with him than I may have mentioned to you. It is true I told him to stop, but I also told him if he didn't, I would advise you to file a suit against him since his descriptions of you were libelous. I also threatened to file a complaint with the ethics board of his discipline, only to find he did not have the necessary credentials to practice. My concern was that such behavior would only encourage the stalking your mother had again initiated, which was relentless and posed a risk to your health and professional status.

In March 2016, my mother called my practice, leaving a message on the office voicemail stating that my brother was dead. He had been found dead by the police, who did a wellness check when he'd failed to respond to my mother's calls. Multiple bowls were found in which my brother had left food and water for his dog. He'd overdosed on the opioid medication he was prescribed for pain. While it was ruled an accident, I believe he died by suicide. The heaviness of that grief is something I cannot find words for. Months passed, during which I could barely get a deep breath – it felt as though I was carrying around a blanket made of lead.

This is what we were addressing in our sessions when the second health scare happened. I believe it was the winter of 2016–2017, though you might be able to correct this timeline. I arrived at your house for our appointment, and there was no answer at the door. By this time, you'd moved your office out of the suite where you'd been seeing patients for some time and were working from your home full time. Because my appointment was at 8:00 a.m., I initially thought you'd overslept. I was less angry with my message, I believe. I remember thinking that I didn't want to do that again – I didn't want to regret being irritated with you because "what if you were really sick again?"

It took about a day or two (the timeline is a bit vague) before I received a call from your wife telling me that you were in the hospital and that it was serious, but she couldn't tell me more because she didn't have any more information to share. She believed she would be able to say more within a few days. When she called back later in the week, she told me that you were recovering and would contact me soon. She also mentioned that you'd asked about me when you'd regained consciousness. She said, "I thought you should know he must have been worried about you."

It turned out you were incorrectly treated after you'd had a minor car accident, Raubolt, but for those first few days, I'd worried you'd had another stroke. When

I saw you again after this episode, I was so angry. I don't know if you knew this, but I was furious with everyone on the planet. I felt so afraid and did not feel like I could tell you this because I knew you weren't having a great time with it all, yourself. I don't remember a lot about that first return session other than feeling really angry and really scared and not believing you when you said you were okay. I did hug you at the end of the session because I'd regretted not doing so when you had the stroke.

It's interesting, Raubolt, how, in the process of writing this book, I see the sequence of things much more clearly than when we were actually going through it. What I am noticing right now is that Matt's death was so close in time to your two medical scares, and I'm wondering how these three events happening in a cluster may have impacted me and my treatment with you.

I've been aware that Matt's death changed things in me. Some of the changes were profound, and some were randomly odd. For example, when he died, I realized for the first time how I might have traveled down the road he did, but I did not. It was a profound change in how I viewed myself. There had been so many points along the way when I could have found myself where he had gone in life. His death made it clear to me that I always made the decision to not only live but to thrive. On the random end of the changes his death created in me was that I could no longer write poetry. Prior to his death, I wrote poetry almost daily. In fact, I worked with a well-respected poet regularly to develop my voice and use of language. So many of those poems were related to my childhood and the experiences I had with Matt that perhaps I shouldn't really be surprised that I stopped having a poetry voice at all when he died.

What I have not been aware of is how your two health scares in close proximity to Matt's death may have changed me and our work together. I wonder if it has made me ambivalent in my attachment to you, though I think I've struggled with attachment all along. I don't know. I do know that the story of your stroke – the false narrative – did truly create an increased consciousness about you as a clinician to other patients and engendered an insecurity that hadn't been there before. What other changes may have occurred as a result of these events is not yet clear to me.

When I proposed writing this book in one of our sessions, Raubolt, I wanted to offer hope to clinicians working with patients with the level of trauma I experienced. I also wanted to document some of the important moments in our work because I believe we co-created something important. I suppose, on some level, I wanted to explore with you why I am doing okay, given all that happened to me. I also wanted to give evidence as to why this kind of therapy needs time – that the depth of this kind of work cannot happen in 12–20 sessions.

I believe I know why insurance companies need to have a sense of the duration of psychotherapy. They have budgets and shareholders to report to. They don't really know how to think about psychotherapy, and I know that the sources they've gone to in order to understand it are academic psychologists. They ask for "standards of care" and "evidence-based treatments" and "measurable outcomes." This is how they do their best for their consumers and their shareholders.

Raubolt's Voice

Rebecca, you are being generous – in my opinion, too generous – in describing the motives and practices of insurance companies. True, they are for-profit businesses and "report" to their shareholders, blah, blah, blah. That is not how they present themselves. They don't give one rip for the welfare of their policyholders. Years ago, I learned from executives of a national, well-known company that it was (is?) standard company policy to delay payment on mental health claims. They discovered that such delays created tension between therapists and their patients, with the end result being treatment was artificially shortened. This practice not only "saved" them money, but they could, in a brazen act of intellectual dishonesty, also claim brief, evidence-based psychotherapy was the new standard of care. This may help explain Shedler's (2018) findings that this touted model has produced remarkably poor results. That they have been aided by the academics in our field having little or no clinical experience only deepens the charade and shame.

I also know that in other countries, psychotherapy is even less available than it is here. Many national health plans only offer short-term, cookie-cutter therapy. So, the fact that insurance companies do cover psychological treatment is helpful to so many who wouldn't be able to access treatment.

Yet, clinicians are under constant threat when they work with insurance companies. They're threatened with audits, with not being paid because of some random rule you didn't realize you were violating, with compensation take backs. Sometimes, you're also told what types of treatments you should be using by a person who has never met your client or the type of outcome measure you should be using to "measure whether therapy is working." These mandates are meant to assure "quality" but often create a sense of dread and fatigue in clinicians that can contribute to resentment and burnout in an already intense profession. And, to put salt in the wound, the insurance plans often pay us significantly less than our fees, meaning we have to see more and more people in order to make an adequate living to pay for student loans and the cost of practicing. Seeing so many clients often isn't psychologically sustainable if you want to do good, deep treatment, so more burnout and more resentment follows, leading clinicians out of the field or toward unwittingly hurting their patients.

I don't have an answer to this conundrum. I know that some clinicians have decided not to take insurance as a means of payment. They only take private pay. Like you, Raubolt, these clinicians feel that dealing with insurance interrupts their work so much that they don't want to deal with it. But, this option limits access to so many people. You kindly worked with me for many years pro bono or at a reduced fee, and I know you've done this for others, as well. But, you can only see so many people this way lest you find yourself in the poor house.

I don't know how this can be addressed, really, but I feel like we, as a profession, need to be constantly considering this dilemma.

I'm aware that many people with my level of childhood trauma, particularly when the trauma reaches into adulthood as mine did, do not thrive. In my roles as clinician, supervisor, and consultant, I've heard about people with less trauma than I experienced struggling to function at all. And, this knowledge has sometimes caused me to question whether I truly am doing okay. I've wondered if perhaps I'm completely unaware of my own psychological wounds. I've wondered if perhaps you, Raubolt, might be blinded to symptoms resulting from my trauma history. Some days, I still wonder about this.

Raubolt's Voice

Rebecca, over the years, you have periodically raised the question of how accurately I was seeing you. There were a number of times you felt I might be "too kind and patient" with you when I should instead have been more confrontational and less understanding. I have never felt that was the correct stance to take with you. To do so seemed like "piling on," adding merit to the harsh, shame-driven self-perceptions you carried. As I see it now, your critical self-assessment cuts toward health as well as away from it. Never letting yourself take the easy road would not allow you to avoid tough decisions or give in to social pressures. In fact, you survived by carving out your own path, which made you different, confusing, and even strange to others, especially growing up. You knew what you didn't want to become and fought tenaciously against it before you were able to define what you aspired to achieve. You had little time or appreciation for quiet reflection, gentleness, or patience with yourself. These experiences you developed through therapy.

I am not without my wounds and tender spots. I still struggle with the fear of people disappearing, and this fear can lead to me leaving relationships before they're done. I can become quite insecure in every single role in my life – mother, psychologist, friend. My hyper-vigilance – the tentacles that Alice Miller and Ward (2008) mention in The Drama of the Gifted Child – gives me way too much information on the moods and words of others, and with that data, I can tell myself that I am being rejected when I might not be.

Yet, I continue to grow and heal, even as a middle-aged woman nearing old age. One area in which I see myself growing is with regard to caring about and honoring myself. On an increasing basis, I'm reminding myself of my own strengths – the things I love about who I am – and trying to spend less time using words that were used against me as a child. It is hard to do, but when I can give myself compassion, and even love, I notice I am better able to navigate difficulties and stress.

Another area where I'm currently growing is in learning to believe in my resilience. Raubolt, over the years, you've often reminded me that while I've struggled, been afraid, and believed all will end when facing painful times, I have not only survived, but I have even grown after these events. For years, your comments about my resilience irked me. I've thought that I haven't grown at all but instead believed that I'm a bit crazier and more fragile after these events. But, recently, I've reflected on all of the moments along the way when I decided to grow instead of die. Like when I decided to apply for and go back to school when the court case first began, and then deciding to move forward when Bob returned even though it meant I would have to face so many demons by doing so. I am a bit crazier, but I suppose one cannot help but go a bit crazy from living.

The most painful and important area where I'm growing is in believing that I matter to others, that I don't disappear for them when I'm not present. This fear impacts so many parts of my life, but most painfully, it creates a sense of aloneness that overwhelms me.

Raubolt's Voice

Rebecca, and so our work together continues but now with greater subtlety and nuance. We talk more about the leading edge, which is where you are going, and less about where you have been.

So, Raubolt, here we are more than 20 years later. Through the "we" of our therapy relationship, I have been able to reclaim so many parts of myself that were terribly wounded by severe, complex childhood trauma that reverberated into my adulthood. It took both of us and the co-created "we" to get me here. I'm grateful to both of us for our willingness to do this work, and I'm curious about where we will find ourselves as we move into this new phase of treatment.

References

Fonagy, P., György, G., Jurist, E., and Target, M. (2018). *Affect Regulation, Mentalization, and the Development of the Self*. Routledge. https://doi.org/10.4324/9780429471643.

Herman, J. (1997). *Trauma and Recovery Aftermath of Violence*. Basic Books.

Joubert, J. (2006). *The Notebooks of Joseph Joubert*. New York Review Books.

Miller, A. and Ward, R. (2008). *The Drama of the Gifted Child: The Search for the True Self*. Basic Books.

Shedler, J. (2018). Where is the evidence for "evidence-based" therapy? *The Psychiatric Clinics of North America, 41*(2), 319–329. https://doi.org/10.1016/j.psc.2018.02.001.

Chapter 8

On the Writing Cure

The following dialogue was based on various guiding questions that spontaneously arose from the original reading of the manuscript and included:

1) What are the implications of what we describe for the practice and interest in psychoanalysis now?
2) To flesh out the questions and dilemmas for therapists who have suffered significant trauma. What responsibility do they have to seek treatment for themselves?
3) What is the role of out-of-office interventions? (wild analysis?)
4) What were the goals of writing this book, and were they accomplished?
5) What were the critical elements of the therapy relationship that made the most impact?
6) Was this book a tribute, and if so, what was the motivation?
7) Is Rebecca "cured," "all better"? Is there such a thing?
8) Loray, what caught your attention? What led you to accept our invitation to participate?

Loray: Rebecca, anytime it's too much, or you feel like "that's enough," we follow you; you are the creator of the work. Dr. Raubolt and Rebecca, I tried to structure the dialogue through five main questions. The questions start rather broadly, and as we explore together, I aim to return to the earlier chapters in more detail. That reflects my reading style, starting more broadly and then tracing the various elements of your written creation. So, I'll start with a space of reflection. Rebecca, I was wondering what it was like for you to create, if not re-create, the psychoanalytic journey from the perspective of both a patient and a clinician now.

Rebecca: So, I wanted to start a little differently, if you don't mind. I wanted to speak briefly about why I proposed this idea to Dr. Raubolt. When I suggested it, I felt a strong desire to address the various things I had heard about people who, like me, have more severe or dramatic trauma histories. To explore what is possible in therapy.

DOI: 10.4324/9781003604723-8

For example, is it possible, in treatment, for someone with such a severe or dramatic trauma to be functioning as well as I am currently functioning? I have heard, in various ways, that if a person has a lot of trauma, they likely would not be doing well. As with my experience with being hospitalized, and at the end of my time there, when the clinician said, "People like you, with that kind of trauma, will be in and out of institutions your whole life." And, as a clinician, I have heard from other clinicians that patients like me, or with this level of trauma, aren't likely going to do well in life and/or in treatment.

With these experiences in mind, I had been reflecting on my treatment with Dr. Raubolt and wondering why I was doing okay. I wondered why I have been able, with struggles, to maintain long-term relationships, be a professional, and to engage in the world that I engage in. Why is that? That was one part of why I wanted to write this book with Dr. Raubolt. I wanted us to explore what we understood about what led to me getting here. I wanted to talk about the process that Dr. Raubolt and I have been able to create. To speak to the parts of both of us that have met and are willing to keep working on things together. With the hope that we, as a profession, might explore what does work and is helpful to people with such trauma.

Loray: Your writing at the beginning of the book speaks to this. You also touch on themes, themes I hope we return to, of how we use language to create categories of distance. It is in the flow of your writing and free associations, especially around pages 4 to 11. You describe how certain types of language and understanding put people at a distance; even well-meaning people can put people at a distance. You also move on to how such languaging and understanding became an internalized form of self-critique; thus, people can become distanced from themselves too! You wrote beautifully about how categories lead to forms of distancing, for example, "damaged beyond repair," "being broken, attention seeking, borderline," and more, needing patients to "file away the ways that I can become needy and empty and bruised as evidence of my brokenness" (Klott et al., 2025, p. 11). And it links with, I think, the second part of your need to write the work – how did you, and how can people with developmental and complex trauma get through life once exposed to such distancing from others? Internalizing something entirely based on distancing rather than contact speaks to your second question: How did you and Dr. Raubolt overcome such developmental traumata, work with such ways of experiencing self and others, and even transcend such ravaging states of mind? Where it's two subjectivities that are important to each other. Mutuality brings in the possibility of good, which is problematic, too, while supporting difference.

Dr. Raubolt also mentioned early in the book that we all have different histories. So there may be distance, but I'm willing to come close. I'm willing to go there with you. I think Grossmark (2018) calls it a psychoanalytic companioning. Some clinicians think that psychoanalysis and therapy, for that matter, is a form of radical friendship or befriending. I just wanted to mention that you wrote beautifully about that segment and its effect on the psyche. So thank you for that.

Rebecca: Part of why I wanted to write about our work together is because I had such a profoundly different experience with Dr. Raubolt, one that I think is important for clinicians to reflect on. *He did not seem to feel bothered, nor did he distance himself from me.* It's something that I've struggled to trust, but this difference has also probably been one of the more healing things about the relationship for me. And, it was unexpected in the writing of this book to see it all on paper.

So, to your original question. I had so many unexpected reactions while writing this book with Dr. Raubolt. I don't know that I understood what I was actually saying we were going to do when I proposed this project. I don't know that I was necessarily psychologically prepared for what this would be like. There were unexpected things – such as reliving some parts that I'd had a long time since last visiting. It was unexpected to feel the closeness with Dr. Raubolt because of our dialogue within the text. I did experience times when I felt like I was pulled back into places that I had long since traveled. It was like returning to a neighborhood you haven't been to for decades and being exposed to all of the things in that neighborhood that you sort of forgot. Well, maybe not forgotten exactly, but you have not thought much about it for years. And yet, what I found really hopeful was how quickly I was able to move through some of that neighborhood. I would be right back in this very painful place, and it would feel terrifying that I would be back there. But it would pass pretty quickly. The feelings of panic or the feelings of sadness or the feelings of rage. I wouldn't stay there for very long, which was nice to see. I wouldn't get lost there; it's just a *haunting*, or a ghost of something.

Loray: Listening to your description, I am reminded of what Meltzer refers to as the function of psychoanalysis: that it can create a sense of buoyancy. One can move into and experience difficult areas yet resurfaces quickly. We are not trapped and swallowed up by those experiences. You know, I love your description, "in the neighborhood." In terms of our developmental architecture, we can "re"-"visit" and see the changes and the haunting. The first image that comes to mind when listening to you was when I visited Germany, on the eastern side, where you can see old buildings that have been renovated but they also still carry the scars of bullet holes. So you get a sense of this newness, but you can feel a history. You also made me think of a spiritual theme of a colleague who walked the Via Dolorosa during a visit to Jerusalem. He sent me a picture of him placing his hand on a handprint on a wall – a sacred symbol, given it is believed that Jesus himself placed his hand on the wall to rest during his walk to Golgotha. To be part of the days leading up to the crucifixion, followed by rebirth. Also, your description of "haunting," which is different from a flashback, illustrates the therapeutic progress.

Rebecca: Thank you. That was the most interesting thing – sometimes, it would feel really raw. As though I wasn't healed, but then I would see my resiliency, so the pain would move through. Because we wrote this while I was still in treatment, we would have sessions during which I would say, "Am I actually any better? Should we abort? Abandon this idea?" And, then, I would be able to process through that and see the resiliency that has developed over time. And this reminded me, as a clinician, of the journey of therapy with the people I was treating. It would remind me that just because we're returning to old places doesn't mean it's a problem. It's a reminder of that part of the process.

This week, one of the people I see said, "You once said that therapy is like a spiral staircase that goes up and up and up. But we come back around, and yet with each time around, we are higher up than we were the last time." I thought, "Oh, I don't remember saying that, but I'll take it." But, this sort of spiral up, and you come back around at a higher place, is what I believe happens in therapy. I probably heard that idea from Dr. Raubolt, or somebody else. And that was helpful as I was writing this, to recognize that recovery or treatment is not a linear sort of process but more of a coming back around to things. And it also helped me remember as a clinician to not lose hope when someone does return to that dark place.

Loray: You reminded me of T.S. Eliot's "Little Gidding" in *The Four Quartets* (Gardners Books; Main edition, April 30, 2001, Originally published 1943), that accentuates a certain approach to life – to not cease from exploration although at the end we may arrive at the very same place we started knowing it anew as if for the first time. Martha Stark also uses similar imagery. The psychoanalyst Cooper (2000) writes about psychoanalysts as *Objects of Hope* – psychoanalysis and psychoanalysts are objects of hope or the surviving object of D.W. Winnicott (Ogden, 2016, 2022). I was thinking of the word *recovery, or* to "re"-cover, the process of being allowed to move back and to be held as analysands creatively *touch* their pain. I recall being an intern and treating people who have had scarring due to burns – the skin changes following their accident. It takes a lengthy rehabilitation process to heal and stretch that skin – developing a new elasticity. But there are many times when the analysand mentioned the skin being too tight, even if they do all the exercises. It's like the skin, our psychic skin, has a life of its own: tightness and full range of motion dialectic. As the treating team, we could not always understand the dialectic as the dialectic was influenced by environmental factors such as temperature changes. Although I don't have direct empirical evidence, it was usually linked to the psyche's stress levels, i.e., their psyche weather and temperatures. Many of the analysands were military, so they weren't interested in the typical talk therapy approach; they wanted more structured exercises and would use that time to both soothe themselves and check in with themselves. Structure served as a stabilizing force, a corset, a brace to brace oneself. Here, I was also reminded of the old Jungian psychoid concept, the unconscious of the unconscious, where body and mind are one, and where psychic vitality comes from and informs the mind-body dialectic/spirals. Rebecca, you also reminded me that we have to look at temporality differently; that's what I hear about where you go in time; it's different for those who have had to deal with too much. Time in trauma works differently. You know, depressive position time, paranoid-schizoid time, and frozen time are all different. I've always been astounded that the mind remembers it as it is now, living in more than one timetable. Of course, I don't want people to live there, as it is highly traumatic to the nervous system. But as an experience, they can travel so quickly within time. I've always been astounded by the capacity of the psyche.

Rebecca: The only other thing that I have reflected on with this book was the noticing of timelines; that was a fascinating experience for me in writing this because I don't know that I realized the timelines when it was happening. Notably, as I say in the last chapter, when I talk about Dr. Raubolt's stroke, my brother's suicide, and then Dr. Raubolt's car accident – how that all came together in time. And how that also coincided with my claim of growth, if that makes sense, my moving into this post-trauma growth. How those events shook some things for me at the time. But, instead of recognizing that growth was happening and had happened, I would say, at the time, there's something wrong with me because I'm having these terrible reactions to all of this. Looking at it from out here, in the writing of this book, allowed me to see all that was happening. I would think, "Oh, wow, what a thing to have had to face. I was able to face all of these very difficult things with resiliency despite the pain and fear."

Then, overarching, the biggest thing, I think, is seeing the relationship between Dr. Raubolt and me in written form. And, this newfound understanding of the relationship that Dr. Raubolt and I have been developing takes us to a different place in treatment. It's taking us to a deeper place but also making me a little bit more vulnerable, I think, over time. So, those are my reactions to your question.

Loray: The work has truly become a transitional object.

Rebecca: Yes, as a matter of fact, when I'm feeling particularly vulnerable, I am now opening the book and finding passages and rereading them to ground myself, which is an interesting thing.

Loray: I did that with my analyst, too. I would go to her words and unique presencing if I was feeling lonely. I also find your thinking on *reclaimed growth* inspiring, especially concerning your description of your eating habits or lack of good eating as a child. I thought, "Oh, your psychic palate is allowing more nourishment. Your psychic taste buds are becoming more alive." Your unique taste and choice of food can, metaphorically speaking, choose/taste your reclamation. A beautiful description that relates to the idea that t, as they say, the proof of the pudding in analysis is how you symbolically worked with the misinformation and gaslighting. But also, reclamation is an alive process; you are choosing, and given the amount of misidentification you experienced, it is worth noting. I also want to link this with Dr. Raubolt and his analyst, Dr. Wolf, who is an excellent self-psychologist. I cannot recall all of his work, but I do recall thoughts like reclamation and restoration of the self.

Dr. Raubolt, if I could move to you for a moment, I would also like to know what it was like for you to read the journey. I found the way you engaged and, at times, suspended yourself as a clinician as both of you were working with a toxic container, toxic paternal containments, groomers, and more. Also, Rebecca was exposed to various males who were clearly unable to serve as creative containers for transformation and protection. They represent the dangerous world; they are predatory objects, as Shrubs (2020) would say, not to mention the psychiatric treatment and opinions that Rebecca had to endure even in her work with you. As her analyst, you had to hold so many spaces and do it eloquently, kindly, and in a transformative paternal way, reminding everyone of the importance of a good father. Also, not just as Rebecca's analyst, but even in Rebecca's work here, you are actively partaking in her "writing cure," an approach I think is unique.

Dr. Raubolt: I wrote out my answer to question one, as I thought that might create some structure for further discussion. When Rebecca approached me about writing the book, I enthusiastically agreed, but not initially. While I was excited about the possibility of such a creative endeavor (I'll defer to your knowledge of the literature), I don't know of any writings like ours where both the analyst-analysand contribute while treatment is ongoing. So it was new territory, clearly, for me. For the first few months, I cautiously observed both of us to see what might become potential difficulties. What I was most worried about and, which turned out to be the most pivotal and creative decision, was the blending of the writing; the back-and-forth dialogue, then the discussion, and some of the emotional repercussions that ensued.

As I read Rebecca's first entry after the introduction, I was convinced again that despite it all, this was a worthwhile project where we were trying to address severe trauma in a much different way, *seeking to describe the process of treatment from the inside out, rather than from the outside in.*

I believe Rebecca described the analytic process well, indicating that the way we spoke and wrote about it in sessions was very similar. We seemed to arrive at similar assessments of the effectiveness of particular interventions. To me, it's like we were speaking the same language, even though I have an analytic language that Rebecca does not. I think that the language that I tried to adopt was more expressive and humanistic than detached and analytical.

Rebecca: Thank God.

Loray: I was thinking similarly.

Dr. Raubolt: What I was unprepared for was the quiet strength, courage, and composure I saw Rebecca express in sessions, and the liveliness of our interaction actually came across on the page. I could feel and see some of the sessions that she described, the conflicts disturbing her life, and her tenacious creativity to live her life more fully. I think Rebecca used the term post-traumatic growth. And I think that is an accurate description. As I understand that term, the emphasis is not on resiliency but on achieving a higher level of development. In other words, it's a huge developmental leap.

It's also striking to me that writing revealed how we were able to blend personal and professional languages. Much like in analysis, I believe I needed to start my writing slowly and tentatively, trying to do my best to follow Rebecca's lead and to adapt to her style of writing. As I became more familiar with the process, these restrictive parameters melted, and I began to respond more spontaneously. Rebecca was able to establish a pace and a style in the writing that deepened our discussion and revealed the treatment process that developed our work together. She presented her history and, in so doing, offered meaningful commentary about how she was coping with the terribly painful experiences she was revealing to me. I could see it at the time. And as I read, I could feel the angst once again as she presented the details about her mother, father, brother, and extended family. I was impressed, and I remain impressed that her writing was so alive with insight and passion. I believe she accurately conveyed what we addressed together for over 20 years, and how, over that period of time, the analytic attitude she developed on the couch could be so effectively presented on the page. Writing about her experiences and analysis with me did not elicit the reservations I first entertained; on the contrary, a deep process for both of us unfolded, providing fresh material for ongoing treatment.

Loray: It's beautifully written, and Rebecca also mentions your ability to feel *into* what is needed and then follow that rhythm, as you did in the writing in-vivo. For me, that is deeply Winnicottian. The unobtrusive relational analysts feel into the other and are able to sense their analysand's *ontological and epistemological needs*. Following the rhythms of the analysand at their own pace enlivens the other. I think many analysands infrequently have had a sustained sense of someone being able to feel into them and hold them and, in time, create an intersubjective space where they can be "enjoyed" based on their own unique creativity. Again, it reminded me of Winnicott (1958, 1963, 1965, 1967, 1969, 1971, 1975) when he wrote about infantile omnipotence; it takes the child a long time to become aware that he did not just create the world he is relating to. But for a very long time, I think many people weren't allowed to create a world for themselves and let the world follow "from" them in a creative way. And from there, slowly but assuredly, be supportively allowed to connect with and have all the disillusionments of life. By having a reliable background of support, as you're writing and your analytic style clearly illustrates, combined with Rebecca's notion of pacing, one remains relatively well protected against intrusion or impingement. Remaining a welcoming other, as in the work of Jeff Eaton and Michael Eigen, is of central importance here. Eaton's work on becoming the welcoming object (2005) and Dr. Eigen's (1985, 1996, 1999, 2001) work on his love of primary process work remind us of what you and Rebecca are describing here – it is a type of work that is very different in structure and process than prevailing models such as CBT where an analysand clocks "in" and "out," come in to "restructure" or be "restructured," versus, allowing someone to be in the "neighborhood" and feel it out and talk about.

Dr. Raubolt: Let me say this: I have a good deal of ambivalence about the designation of non-obtrusive analyst. I understand the history, particularly Balint's contributions, and I appreciate the emotional growth that such an approach can inspire. I also believe that I was active regarding my personal engagement with Rebecca and my reactions to what she was talking about, both professionally and personally.

I did not always extend my activity; if it was silently expressed, she could still feel it or perhaps sense my reaction would be more accurate. Rebecca often knew when I was moved or angered about the violence of the abuse she was describing. And so, I think this type of engagement, while it risks having troubling countertransferential components, was the glue that helped us open up more and more of Rebecca's history and experientially go through the remaining difficulties, wounds, and history so that it was more than cognitive exercise. I wasn't simply explaining or offering an interpretation and then *stepping back*; instead, I often used interpretations *to step into the relationship* and bring the immediacy of my presence into focus.

Loray: I think it is a significant differentiation. And I couldn't help but think that your way of holding the distinction is similar to the work of the well-known Sullivanian Dr. Leston Havens and his book *A Safe Space* (1989). As a Sullivanian, he mentions the importance and difficulty of stepping into an engagement versus, at that time, the tendency to explain or interpret-only approach. He mentions he did not find the latter helpful. Rebecca, before I move on, is there anything that you'd like to add to that or something that came up for you?

Rebecca: As I explained in the book, I'm not trained as a psychoanalyst. And so the concept of how much to stay out or be in the field or any of that, I don't know, and I don't have an academic response to it. But what I can *say as the analysand* is that had there not been moments where I could tell that Dr. Raubolt was entering-in, I don't know that I could have done half of the work that I've done. Nor would I have been able to express half of the emotion because I would have felt too alone. Sometimes, when going through this level of trauma, again, to have to say it again to somebody else but do that alone. . . . Perhaps some people can do that, but I could not have. In some ways, his entering the field, I think I'm using that phrase correctly, *he loaned me enough of himself to get through it, if that makes sense.*

Loray: That's lovely.

Rebecca: Do you want me to continue? Okay, because your next question was about writing. You asked, "Writing was part of your journey from a young age. And authoring seems vital to connect with both yourself and others. Could you say more about that?" When reflecting on your question, I realize that I started writing as a child. I had a fantasy. As a fairly young child, I had a fantasy about being a writer. The characters in movies or in books who were writers were the most attractive characters to me. For example, in *Little Women*, Jo is the writer, and she is the most interesting, relatable character in the book for me. Looking back, the writing characters are the characters that can understand what's happening and give words to the events around them. And, I think they also are the people who make sense of everything. They make sense of their worlds. And it seemed vital to me that I would be that character. So, as a child, that was my fantasy, that I would be that *character observing and making sense of this world that I was in.* I think it probably was a way for me to distance myself from the trauma and from what was happening. I think, if I had this fantasy, "I'm the writer of this world; I'm writing about what's happening," it gave me some space and gave me a chance to make sense through that writing and to buffer me in some ways.

When I started to see Dr. Raubolt, one of the things that was really quite moving was he was interested in what I was writing. He was very generous in that he would be willing to read what I wrote fairly early on, and he was supportive of it. So, it was a way for me to share this thing that I had done throughout my life, the writing. It also made me feel like what I was writing or what I had to say mattered. I think a lot of times in my past when I would try to share what I was writing with a clinician they would see it as a bother of some kind or an avoidance perhaps. I'm not really sure what they were feeling, but Dr. Raubolt's willingness again to enter the field, to let me send him poetry, to let me send whatever number of things, was pretty important.

Loray: "Writing-as-cure" expressions. Apologies for interrupting you there; this is very important to you. Your writing is very important; it shines through. I am also reminded of "negative distance," how we as clinicians have created a language that has not really helped people always get in contact with themselves. But it is important to remember, as Michael Eigen writes, that we have a talking cure and a writing cure. Writing can be extremely curative as it could support a "creative distance." So it seems with your writing. I didn't think of it until now, how writing in therapy was used in a binary way. Your description taps into the reality that it served a creative function – providing a bit of time to reflect, enabling processing capacities, having food for thought, and using the mind as a digestive tract so that we can work through experiences. Some clinicians, such as Susan Kavaler-Adler, have writing groups to work through developmental mourning constellations. I think it was Irving Yalom who would write to everyone after his group sessions about the process. Christopher Bollas has a word for it; he calls it the *lucid object* in his book *Catch Them Before They Fall* (2013). As part of the therapy, specifically after a painful but needed regression, he would provide the analysand with a written representation of how he understood the process. It served as orientation, memory, and a holding and containing activity. So, it seems your writing is in the tradition of the lucid object, writing as providing creative distance to make sense of that which is chaotic and does not have helpful external objects. These transformative objects can help us narrate it in a way that is, again, of importance process-wise. Dr. Raubolt would accept it and take in your creations.

Dr. Raubolt: I think Rebecca's poetry, in particular, was experience-near, and, therefore, a continuation rather than a resistance to disclosure. I believe it also provided an additional advantage in the sense that it allowed her to express emotions, thoughts, and even historical images, but through the structure of poetry, it was also contained. To my way of thinking, it was an extension of the therapy process of opening, expressing, and containing, which, in turn, helped develop emotional self-regulation. I did not see her writing as resistance; I saw it as a deepening of the analytic process. In other words, I recalled that in Freud's age he took analysands on vacations or other forms of extending sessions. This I saw as an extension of the therapy, much like an extended session where Rebecca would take something, and work it and work it and rework it. And it would be transformative in the process.

Rebecca: And, there, just now, this conversation, in real-time, is reworking something for me. The idea that what I have to say, or what I was doing, was good and important versus taking a lot of attention. It challenges a lot of messages from early life about my wanting to be seen and the idea that to express something was seen as negative, or needy, or too much. And instead, the willingness of Dr. Raubolt to see it for what it was, what I wanted it to be seen for, which was, "I'm trying, I'm trying here to keep working with you, I'm trying to keep being in relationship with you" through my writing. So even now, in that real-time, there are different ways of seeing it. I believe it is part of what Dr. Raubolt was talking about, as far as entering in and not standing outside the field.

Loray: Rebecca, as you were explaining, I was thinking of "corrective experiences" one could have in analysis. This starkly contrasts with your previous experiences – of how your way and being was interpreted negatively. Think, for example, of descriptions such as "attention seeking," being "too needy," or writing as resistance only, combined with categories as being borderline and acting out. Your work with Dr. Raubolt and his understanding contextualizes the differences very quickly and firmly about what it is and what it is not. Similar to the book volume by Jeffrey Seinfeld, *Interpreting and Holding: The Paternal and Maternal Functions of the Psychotherapist* (1993), Dr. Raubolt's *way of both* maternally holding and paternally differentiating what it is and what it is not, I find it very helpful – especially if one has been exposed to a world of chaos. To know what it is and what it's not. It creates safety and supports therapeutic play, working against feelings of isolation and exile. . . . Dr. Raubolt, I was also thinking now about the various mediums you use to represent what is difficult and even vilified. Your work as a filmmaker on *Detroit Living in Between, Art as Medicine, Stories Beneath the Skin, Heidelberg 360,* and more recently, *The Accomplice,* brings across a welcoming aesthetic and an ability to narrate areas that could be seen as dark or difficult; finding, if not creating, visual containers for "dark" areas. I was wondering about that, combined with the work that both you and Rebecca are bringing "into various neighborhoods," so to speak. Rebecca's capacity as a writer, creator, and observer, as well as something that you share with her. If I can be so bold as to say something that your creative souls have in common – a shared creative spark. I just wanted to bring those parts of your creativity as an artist in as well, not just as an elder in the field, but also as an artist that creates for others, as writers do; leaving objects of reflection for us, aesthetic repositories that can make entering difficult fields of experience easier. So I was wondering if you could say something about that part of you?

Dr. Raubolt: Since you brought up films, let me start there. I thank you for the generous designation. As a filmmaker, I think I come up with ideas, fund them, and provide the interviews and context while leaving all the technical challenges to other people. I remember, though, that with the first film, Detroit Living In Between, the editor wanted me to write a voiceover to begin the film. I wrote about two pages, which I was quite pleased with. In fact, I thought it was some of my best writing because it was very expressive and creative. Yet, a week later, when I returned, he handed me an edited version of what I had written. It was reduced to about five or six lines, so I asked, "What, you don't like the way I write?" He, in return, emphasized a very important lesson that I had forgotten. He said, "I don't want to hear it; I want to see it. I want your words to come alive on the screen to pull me into it, not to tell me about something." Those words changed the way that I began viewing films as well as the type of films I subsequently made. It also confirmed my professional writing. Since finishing graduate school, I've written a lot about my clinical experiences initially to see what it was that I thought, to put it on paper, and to see if I could, in a reflective, knowledgeable way, conceptualize what it was that I was doing during the treatment hour. As time went on, that changed from figuring out what I wanted to do to understanding what others were writing and the thoughts I had about what they were writing. Now, initially, I was writing not in my own language, as it were; I was writing in what I imagined was analytic style. I have been around and in psychoanalysis for a very long time, but I've always been an outsider. I didn't go to an APA-approved psychoanalytic Institute. I'm not part of one now. And the criticism that I will hear about my writing is that it's more of a presentation than an article. And I take that as a compliment, but I don't think it was meant that way.

It wasn't until I became involved with IFPE, the International Forum for Psychoanalytic Education, that I found people who write the way that I do, which, again, is more experiential. I went so far as to make a presentation entitled "Writing analytically without inducing psychic sleep." Much of psychoanalytic writing can be pedantic conservative and, as a result, tiresome. Frequently, journal articles are weighted down with obtuse or stultifying language, while personal and intimate writings are usually sanitized or dismissed to keep the subversive nature of psychoanalysis muted. So, I've been drawn more to novelists in terms of my writing style, and in fact, I believe there were about four or five years when I read only novelists because I felt that their use of language was more akin to what I understood and appreciated. I also thought that they offered more textured presentations of characters than anything I was reading in analytic texts. That's not to say that is universally true. I believe Michael Eigen, Allen Wheelis, Jeff Eaton, and Christopher Bollas, in particular, have this sensuous prose that I think addresses the analytic, creative, and personal (autobiographical reflections) while breathing some life into our field. I believe without such voices, we run the risk of becoming obsolete. I don't think some of the definitions of what it means to practice psychoanalytically or to write psychoanalytically are particularly helpful. They are often too constraining and drowning in orthodoxy or burdened with obscure references and arcane theories. By contrast, I think that my writing has allowed for the personal expression of what I am most drawn to analytically. I'm now venturing into shorter fiction, especially dark flash fiction because I think different, evocative voices need to be heard. I guess that is also one of the trademarks of my films, whether it be on Detroit or LGBTQ reactions to the Trump administration or piercings and tattoos. Each looks at what is implicit in these experiences and how people construct points of self-reference. *The purpose is not to pathologize but to hear how voices reveal who one is and where one is going.* Extending this process to analysis, I listen for the whispers reflecting the inside world being created.

Loray: As you were talking, I was aware of so many parallels with Rebecca's story. Again, I mean the reference to *language that distances*, the reality of experience-distant language, and psychoanalytic techniques that distance. It doesn't help nor make people feel connected, leaving them feeling like outsiders. This stands in contrast with allowing expression of self and the importance of creativity: growth and creativity evoked from the inside growing outwards, necessitating a sensitivity to the psyche's whispers, as you mention.

Dr. Raubolt: You know, I was thinking as you're talking about that one word we didn't use in the book, but it describes what you are articulating just now, which is *mutuality*. I think we've talked about it without using that word. I'm not sure how we managed to do that. Maybe there's an association to mentioning Ferenczi (1988) and his experiments. Nonetheless, I think there was a mutually collaborative process where the analysis was changing both of us.

Loray: Yes. You mentioned it in the work as well. It's not just the analysand that changes; the analysis also changes the analyst. There is a mutuality there. And it is interesting, as you were speaking about it, my eye caught a book by Hoffman with the title "Towards Mutual Recognition" (2010). A rich volume in the tradition of Ferenczi. He brings into view the creative interaction between Ferenzci and his analysands, who themselves became significant contributors – a kind of spiritual connection. Think here of Elizabeth Severn (2017) and Izette de Forest's "Leaven of Love" (1954). It is sensing something deeper, elements of how people change each other in a soulful way. And thank God for people like Michael Eigen (1985, 2001) who are willing to write about this and suffer the critique that comes with it. But it is mutual.

Okay. I'm going to jump to question three. Rebecca, we are reading about your journey not only from your psychoanalytic years but also throughout. What have been the aspects that keep growth going? And how has your psychoanalytic process informed or supported the latter? You touch upon some of it, your ability to be a writer.

Rebecca: I have to tell you that this was probably the most challenging question for me to answer. I spoke about it with my friend and said, "I could say the truth of what I think, but I'm not sure that this is the answer he is looking for." The best that I could come up with was, again, a fantasy from childhood that carried me through. There was a book that I read as a fairly young person called "A Little Princess." I don't know if you know the context of this story. But basically, it begins with a little girl raised by a wealthy father, and he puts her into a boarding school in the UK. Pretty quickly after she is left there, her father dies, and she's left destitute and is treated terribly by the people meant to care for her.

Throughout the book, she's tempted with giving up, with doing bad things, but she decides that she wants to be better, to do the right thing, to be good. And because of that, she finds true friends and is eventually rescued by a wealthy family who discovers her true identity. She's rescued. It was a very powerful book, in my mind, as a child. I think that what I took from it was this belief that it's very important that I keep trying, and that I keep working at things, to keep growing. Because it would matter. It would matter if I kept trying to do better, be a decent person. Later, when I found my way into this church, there was a reinforcing of that idea, that it was important that I continue to try, to do right. I received a strong message that something good would come if I kept trying and growing. And, then later, in treatment with Dr. Raubolt, in particular, I think I found that if I kept trying, and I kept working at it, that there could indeed be a rescue from the pain. And so, I suppose, I think there may have been some fantasy about it mattering; it mattered whether or not I kept trying and kept growing. And Dr. Raubolt actually seemed to collude with me on that. He joined with me in that belief that it is important that I survive and grow.

Additionally, I think that there's always been another part of me that has rebelled against my history. There has been a pushing against where I came from as a standard from which I wanted to go away from. I'm not sure if that was answering your question, but that's what came to my mind.

Loray: I'm deeply touched by your story. You had an *organizing mythology* through literature, which clearly helped your internal world. It was something, again, that goes both ways. I think it helped, but your psyche was seeking it, and found it. The book resonated with your internal capacities. You know, if we were tabula rasa, we would say stories create us. I think we seek stories. You remind me of a book I love too by Agnès de Lestrade-Phileas's *Fortune: A Story About Self-Expression*. I was deeply touched by your story. To me, it made so much sense that your preconceptions, the parts of you, that are you, could find a cultural representation that could provide vitality, structure, and hope. So I couldn't have asked for a better answer.

Rebecca: Really? I was not sure how to answer that.

Loray: I think Antonia Ferro, the Italian psychoanalyst, was the one I was thinking of when Dr. Raubolt was talking about different ways of trying to keep analysis alive. He relies on literature and media as a field theorist. He also worked with children initially, which may have contributed to his novel approaches. He was influenced by Robert Lang's work on the bipersonal field and the adaptive context. Ferro makes use of the latter and includes movies, books, etc., within the psychic field as objects of vitality. Given the latter, if an analysand thus talks about movies, much can be gained from it – that is, which genre is the analysand bringing into the field currently, and possibly, how does it serve as an expression of self and others? And much more! Given the "A Princess" story – there was something in that story of a loss of hope, of finding meaning anew that you also spontaneously found in the external world with religion. I think kids have a spiritual core.

Rebecca: Books, television, and movies were how I was raised. I learned about families and how families could be from books or on television.

Loray: You knew what to look for. Meltzer uses Winnicott to say we gather the transference, don't say things too quickly, we gather over time. But I also think what you're reminding me of this gift is how people gather "health" through images and stories and TV programs, and these were parts of you that saw it in the world and sought that and knew there was something better I think that would Dr. Eigen will call analytic Faith. Something can get better. It transcends hope; it's a core thing. Dr. Raubolt, given the process, what are your thoughts on the healing factors in psychoanalysis? And why is it important to talk more openly about it? After I read it, I thought I had given you an extremely difficult question.

Dr. Raubolt: I think it's important to talk about the person of the analyst. We have many theoretical formulations about the patients and a lot about diagnostic criteria. And a lot about our favorite concepts, which change over time, but plenty of material. I think we need to talk about the person of the analyst because, increasingly, I believe it's the relationship that is the curative container through which the analytic process unfolds. So, I think it's easier to describe what the healing relationship is. I made a list of some that came to mind, so I'll start with authenticity and genuine concern and then add love, emotional presence, honesty, capacity to make and acknowledge mistakes, responsiveness, creativity, emotional aliveness, and from my Portuguese colleagues I have come to appreciate the twin process of courage and vulnerability that go with being an analyst. I said earlier that I don't believe that change can occur without both parties, analyst and patient, changing. I also see that the analyst's change must precede the patient's. I don't think, in my experience anyway, that patients will go where the analyst hasn't already been. In the process, the analyst listens, observes, becomes aware of, joins with, and, through past experiences, the subtle changes and shifts generated in the process and through the patient are fed back in unconscious ways to the patient. So it's a back and forth, sometimes recognized consciously, sometimes largely unconsciously, where words need to be found, hopefully not bought but found.

On the other hand, notice the factors I did not include, which seem to be what we have become enamored with in defining analysis like the use of the couch, the number and frequency of sessions. I can borrow from Jonathan Shedler (2006) for a moment. He writes at the risk of offending some psychoanalysts. A few words of definition are in order about psychoanalysis; it is an interpersonal process, not an anatomical position. It refers to a special kind of interaction between patient and therapist. Lying down and meeting frequently are only the trappings of psychoanalysis, not the essence. I think it was Gill (1983) who said, with respect to the frequency of meaning of meetings, it's silly to maintain that someone who attends four appointments per week is in psychoanalysis, but someone who attends only three cannot be; some attend their sessions only once or twice a week, as was the case with Rebecca. Sit in a chair, which essentially was the way therapy was often conducted. Not always, as there was a period of time with the couch. And there's no question that either way, the analytic process was taking place in my mind. It really has to do with who the therapist is, who the patient is, and what happens between them. Within that context, the unconscious was clearly acknowledged, as were resistances and transferences, and dream material was also very much present. But again, it's in an alive process, with more fluidity and engagement rather than distance and explanation. I know for myself that I had the experience of being in an analysis with Ernest Wolf, and I would meet with him for a double session.

Then, we would walk together to Chicago Institute for a two-hour seminar he co-taught with Marion Tolpin. There was this blending of experiences, where I could be the analysand with him and have his exclusive attention within that framework, go through the analytic process; there was then a collegial connection as we walked the few blocks over to the institute where he would tell me about his life and we would engage in discussion. When the seminar/supervision started, he was the teacher, and I was in student mode because he blended both. There was this very nice flow back and forth. Marian Tolpin gave another example of similar flexibility. When she was in analysis with Kohut, she also wanted to learn about self-psychology (she was one of that initial group of eight). So when she wanted analytic treatment, she would lie on a couch, and when she wanted to talk to him about a case, she would sit up on the couch. It was his back and forth and use of the couch in a much different way. I think again about the ability and flexibility to shift roles to make space without contaminating the necessary requirements for therapy. I think this is an area where something needs to be developed, not something that is wildly unorthodox and, therefore, viewed with suspicion.

Loray: I greatly appreciate the way you mentioned that flow and how the parameters are the frames of the context that hold and create their own content in a helpful way. The psyche can then move between different contexts, with greater fluidity rather than things becoming rigid, stultifying, or an argument about what is Orthodox and not. When it comes to human experience, you remind me that a very similar process would occur when Guntrip was in an analysis with Fairbairn (Guntrip, 1975). Guntrip would start with a couch session, and then afterward, they would talk about the process and psychoanalytic theory. I think it supported Guntrip's ability to be a writer, a scholar, and a compassionate human being. Dr. Eigen himself said, you know, some people he sees on the couch some once a week, twice a week, sometimes more, sometimes less, and to him, it's analysis; he doesn't make that distinction for himself anymore. It's the contact, it's analytic contact. For him, I think that's what I take from you.

Dr. Raubolt: When I first met with Wolf for a consultation, I told him I was interested in self-psychological-based analysis. He met with me and, at the end of the consultation hour, said, "I believe that I can help you find a good analyst." I thanked him and rather sheepishly said, "That'd be fine, except I want you." And I'm in Michigan, you're in Chicago, and there really is no feasible way that I can afford the time or the expense of three to four times a week, which is what I think he was seeing people then, he looked at me, and he paused for a moment and said, "I guess we'll have an unorthodox analysis then." Within that process, there were a couple of things that he said along the way that really made a significant difference to me personally, but also professionally. Most of all, he displayed a willingness to meet me where I was, not where theory or the teaching said I should be. He was, I think, 78 at the time, and he considered himself an unreconstructed rebel even as he was classically trained. However, the theory did not get in the way of his being with people. It informed him, but it did not ultimately define him.

Loray: There's so much to connect to here, but before I continue, I want to hear from Rebecca what she is hearing. I love these descriptions – willing to meet me where I was, being an unreconstructed rebel, reconstructing for you what you need. It seems something of Dr. Wolf was carrying on through you and then through to Rebecca, as well.

Rebecca: I think that's what happens with clinicians. We carry what our clinicians give to us. We carry them out into the world of our patients. I can't express how much Dr. Raubolt has influenced me as a clinician and the way that I think about things. I also want to just say that I find it unfortunate that the rules around psychoanalytic and the psychoanalytic world are so restrictive regarding what constitutes psychoanalysis. I don't know how many times I've come into Dr. Raubolt's office and said, "Am I in analysis? I'm not sure I'm in analysis because I just read this thing about analysis that says that maybe I'm not in analysis. And does that mean you don't think I'm good enough for analysis? Do you think I'm not well enough for analysis? Is that what's happening there?"

Also, I probably would have become an analyst if it was something that was accessible to somebody who doesn't have a financial background to do all of the training and the requirements. I don't think that it should get watered down necessarily, but there would be no way that I could ever afford four or five times a week of psychoanalysis. It's just not possible. I do think that it is limiting the younger generation.

Loray: I think it's about how we keep things that are creative, alive, and accessible. It may be good to revisit the history of the growth of psychoanalysis and its becoming Institutionalized. Kernberg (2016), Civitarese (2024), Raubolt (2006), Kirsner (2009), and many others have written about modern-day complexities and the lack of accessibility and innovation.

Dr. Raubolt: If I'm not mistaken, I think Freud made one reference to multiple sessions per week and phrased it as advice. Somehow, that has been translated into this arbitrary structure. One reason this occurred was to distinguish analysis from psychotherapy; as you know, Loray, immigrant analysts from Europe came after the war. They wanted to separate themselves from women and lay-analysts, so they tightened up the requirements and restricted admission to training institutes. I believe Brill founded the New York Psychoanalytic Institute around this time, the most prestigious and influential analytic institute in America, and they admitted only medical doctors for training.

Loray: Only medical doctors. This is a reason why brilliant scholars like Eric Fromm eventually had to leave the William Alanson White Institute and relocate to New Mexico. So there's a lot of politics. And Dr. Raubolt, it's good to know where we come from. When Freud started psychoanalysis, the frame was very different from what is seen today – even the great Robert Langs adapted the frame to fit his communicative approach, that is, 90-minute sessions, 45 minutes of free association, and the other 45 minutes was a form of interpreting the adaptive context, which is a form of education, about the content, to get to work with the unconscious material and the transference. It was his way of working. So, he found his own way of working. Rebecca, I think a part of me is just so identifying – the theme of exclusion, not being seen, and more. And it links with our later questions in the field, how people left feeling not enough, even with PhDs, when it comes to treating other people, but if you're not CBT, you're not empirical, which is absolute nonsense. And I'll link it in my last chapter. Maybe the last question for the day – Rebecca, as you were listening to what Dr. Raubolt was saying, I wondered what was coming up for you. You're a clinician and an analysand, and you've been through training, but you're also a service user.

Rebecca: For some of them, it's a point of pride. In my experience, as a supervisor, one of the most disturbing things I have heard is statements such as "I have never had any treatment," but "Isn't that a great thing that I've never needed any treatment?" It's something that I try to disabuse them of very quickly. I don't know how universal my experience of graduate school is, so I don't want to make sweeping comments, but in my training, there was a very strong message from some of my professors that if you had something wrong with you in any way that would mean you would need treatment, you should not be a treating clinician. It was so distressing to me, which is another part of why I wanted to write about this. It was what led to my doctoral dissertation topic. I think that it must have something to do with the medical model concept of psychotherapy that's been happening increasingly over the last 30 years. This is just my thinking; I have no citations whatsoever. This is only my thinking. That, the idea of a medical model, means something like, "If you go to psychotherapy, there's something wrong with you medically." And this gives the impression to clinicians that they don't want to be seen that way; they don't want to be thought of in those terms. And so, to go into therapy would mean I was acknowledging that there's something wrong with me medically. The other part that I think a lot about is that the education around conceptualization and understanding the human experience is becoming dumbed down to such an extent that clinicians don't believe that anybody is really going to understand what's happening for them, if they do go to see someone.

I earned my Master's degree in the '90s and then my doctorate 11 years later, and I believe there was a significant dumbing down in the depth of the education regarding psychotherapy from my masters to my doctorate. In my Master's, I at least learned about Winnicott. I learned about deeper thought in some ways, but some professors made fun of this type of depth in my doctorate training. Some of my faculty were able to explore attachment, but most wanted us to focus solely on cognitive restructuring without understanding how "faulty cognitions" are formed or why they're in use by our patients. If I had been a clinician who had only learned during my doctoral studies, I would not have believed that psychotherapy had much to offer me.

Loray: This is an important theme in your writing and also Dr. Raubolt's thinking and sensitive response to what the analysand brings. The current clinical and medical models, important as they are, are wholly insufficient to account for the depth and complexity of being fully human. Listening to an individual with "symptoms" often, I remain astounded that they are doing a wonderful job under very complex inner and outer realities. The jump to the medical model and medicalization of all human suffering is coming under scrutiny as it has had a real-life fallout for many – a reality Rebecca writes about. Add other contexts, such as the law, and it's a wonder people survive their own traumas.

Dr. Raubolt: Loray, as you were talking, I was thinking about the Guntrip article you summarized. There was a quote that caught my attention and resonated with my sensibility. I am paraphrasing Winnicott, but he wrote something like, "We differ from Freud. He was for curing symptoms; we are concerned about the person's whole living and loving."

Loray: That's beautiful. Thank you very much.

Bibliography

Bollas, C. (2013). *Catch Them before They Fall*. Routledge.

Civitarese, G. (2024). *On Arrogance: A Psychoanalytic Essay*. Routledge.

Cooper, S. H. (2000). *Object of Hope-Exploring Possibility and Limit in Psychoanalysis*. The Analytic Press.

De Forest, I. (1954). *The Leaven of Love: A Development of the Psychoanalytic Theory and Technique of Sandor Ferenczi*. Harper and Brothers.

Eaton, J. E. (2005). The obstructive object. *Psychoanalytic Review*, *92*(3), 355–372.

Eigen, M. (1985). Toward Bion's starting point: Between catastrophe and faith. *International Journal of Psychoanalysis*, *66*, 321–330.

Eigen, M. (1996). *Psychic Deadness*. Jason Aronson, Inc.

Eigen, M. (1999). *Toxic Nourishment*. Karnac.

Eigen, M. (2001). *Damaged Bonds*. Karnac.

Ferenczi, S. (1988). *The Clinical Diary of Sándor Ferenczi*. Edited by J. Dupont. Translated by M. Balint and N. Z. Jackson. Harvard University Press.

Gill, M. M. (1983). The point of view of psychoanalysis: Energy discharge or person? *Psychoanalysis & Contemporary Thought*, *6*(4), 523–551.

Grossmark, R. (2018). *The Unobtrusive Relational Analyst: Explorations in Psychoanalytic Companioning*. Routledge.

Guntrip, H. (1975). My experience of analysis with Fairbairn and Winnicott – (how complete a result does psycho-analytic therapy achieve?). *International Review of Psychoanalysis*, *2*, 145–156.

Havens, L. (1989). *A Safe Space: Laying the Groundwork of Psychotherapy*. Harvard University Press.

Hoffman, M. T. (2010). *Toward Mutual Recognition: Relational Psychoanalysis and the Christian Narrative*. Routledge.

Kernberg, O. F. (1996). Thirty methods to destroy the creativity of psychoanalytic candidates. *International Journal of Psychoanalysis*, *77*(5), 1031–1040.

Kernberg, O. F. (2016). *Psychoanalytic Education at the Crossroads: Reformation, Change and the Future of Psychoanalytic Training*. Routledge.

Kirsner, D. (2009). *Unfree Associations: Inside Psychoanalytic Institutes*. Jason Aronson, Inc.

Ogden, T. (2016). *Reclaiming Unlived Life*. Routledge.

Ogden, T. (2022). *Coming to Life in the Consulting Room*. Routledge.

Raubolt, R. (2006). *Power Games*. Other Press.

Seinfeld, J. (1993). *Interpreting and Holding: The Paternal and Maternal Functions of the Psychotherapist*. Jason Aronson, Inc.

Severn, E. (2017). *The Discovery of the Self: A Study in Psychological Cure*. Edited by P. L. Rudnytsky. Routledge.

Shedler, J. (2006). That was then, this is now: Psychoanalytic psychotherapy for the rest of us. http://jonathanshedler.com/writings/.

Winnicott, D. W. (1958). The capacity to be alone. *International Journal of Psychoanalysis*, *39*, 416–420.

Winnicott, D. W. (1963). Communicating and not communicating leading to a study of certain opposites. In L. Caldwell and H. T. Robinson (Eds.) (2016), *The Collected Works of D. W. Winnicott: Volume 6, 1960–1963*, Chapter 8 (pp. 433–446). Oxford University Press.

Winnicott, D. W. (1965). *The Maturational Processes and the Facilitating Environment*. Hogarth.

Winnicott, D. W. (1967). The location of cultural experience. *International Journal of Psychoanalysis*, *48*, 368–372.

Winnicott, D. W. (1969). The use of an object. *International Journal of Psychoanalysis*, *50*, 711–716.

Winnicott, D. W. (1971). *Playing and Reality*. Routledge.

Winnicott, D. W. (1975). *Through Pediatrics to Psychoanalysis*. Hogarth.

Chapter 9

On Ontological Survival and the Children of the Second Birth

But, when I met you, parts of me were also certain I was beyond repair. That it was just a matter of time before you, too, would know that I was a shattered person. That I was broken. And, worse, that I was despicable and needed to be avoided at all costs.

(Klott et al., 2025, p. 13)

Psychoanalysis as Writing Cure – On Mutuality and the Creation of Lucid Objects

For those fortunate to have experienced a transformative analysis, words alone cannot convey the healing potential and support of life-affirming ways of being-in-the-world that an analysis can provide. More than being a *talking cure* exclusively, it was Bertha Pappenheim, one of the originators of the psychoanalytic method, who also used psychoanalysis as a *writing cure*. In the current work, Drs Raubolt and Klott faithfully invite the reader into both psychoanalytic mediums, the private room of the psychoanalytic hour, and the mutuality found in the psychoanalytic dialogue within the written medium. Their work continues a rich and growing tradition as seen in various psychoanalytic texts such as Simley Blanton's *Diary of My Analysis with Sigmund Freud* (1971), Harry Guntrip's *My Experience of Analysis with Fairbairn and Winnicott* (1975), Tilman Moser's *Years of Apprenticeship on the Couch: Fragments of My Psychoanalysis* (1977), Richard Reichbart's *Anatomy of a Psychotic Experience* (2022), Dörte von Drigalski's *Flowers on Granite* (1979), George Eastman's *Freeing the Imprisoned Self: A Memoir* (2014), Annita Perez Sawyer's *Smoking, Cigarettes, Eating Glass: A Psychologists Memoir* (2015), Annie Rogers' *A Shining Affliction* (1995), *The Unsayable: The Hidden Language of Trauma* (2006), and *Incandescent Alphabets: Psychosis and the Enigma of Language* (2016), R.E. Rothenberg's *The Jewel in the Wound: How the Body Expresses the Needs of the Psyche and Offers a Path to Transformation* (2001), and many more from esteemed psychoanalysts such as Wilfred Bion (1990), Michael Eigen (1986, 1992, 1995, 1999, 2001, 2004, 2007, 2018), and Henry Parens (2004). I remain grateful for their various *aesthetic*

DOI: 10.4324/9781003604723-9

and *lucid objects* (Bollas, 2013) created for further dialogue and reflection. In the words of Dr. Klott:

> As Dr. Raubolt and I worked on this project, *we knew we wanted to invite you,* the reader, into our clinical hours. So, in this spirit, we now ask you to join us in viewing, unvarnished and raw, what treatment is like for both the severely traumatized patient and the clinician tasked with helping the patient work toward healing.

Also,

> If you are not a survivor of complex trauma, this approach could allow you to grasp the patient's healing experience more viscerally than is often possible when only hearing from the clinician's point of view. If you have sustained complex trauma, our hope is that you will see, through reading about my journey, that you are not alone nor beyond help and that there are clinicians willing and able to journey with you.
>
> (Klott et al., 2025, pp. xii, xiii; italics added)

Rumi's Guest House "for" Our Gone Children

Being invited by Dr. Raubolt to engage with the written work of Dr. Klott touched me in innumerable ways and re-evoked long-forgotten memories of being lost and found. Dr. Klott's heartfelt writing, her creative reliance, and her use of a cherished childhood book[1] (*A Little Princess* by Frances Hodgson Burnett) touched my own experiences of psychological survival and a sense of *autonomy in extreme situations* (Marcus, 1999). Even more so, a deep gratitude for those "objects" and "people" who served as lucid and welcoming others in lives characterized by the painful vicissitudes of absence (Williams, 2010, 2013, 2022). Attempting a selection to convey the impact and importance of Dr. Klott's and Raubolt's work remains difficult as so many vertices are possible. A choice remains necessary, and given the powerful theme of *absence* in Dr. Klott's work, I bring her work in relationship with that of psychoanalyst Paul Williams, especially his concept of *Gone Children*.

On Paul William's *The Authority of Tenderness*

"Gone" and "Return" (rebirth), the infinitesimal and immutable variations and permutations of "gone" and "return," both qualitatively and quantitatively different from "lost and found" (although included in such rhythms), find creative expression in the work of Paul Williams. Through three small volumes entitled, *The Fifth Principle* (2010), *Scum* (2013), and *The Authority of Tenderness* (2022), Williams writes on the *Gone Child* and the various strands of humanity needed to engage, if not to bring to life, such a child from living outside the orbit of others. My current writing cannot do justice to William's exceptional rendering of the inner world and experience of Gone Children. I can but provide a few descriptions as reveries and thicken it through Dr. Klott's writing:

> I find myself rudderless, imperceptibly small, and taken to a place where all that is inside me seems to be emptied out. . . . This emptying out may have come to define me. It became more familiar to me than any other state of mind I know. Insubstantial, without redemption and filled with dread, I became alien, on the verge of disappearing, unable to think, speak or help myself.
>
> (Williams, 2010, p. 12)

*****

> The woods was my childhood sanctuary; my place, with what seemed to be a familiar but inexhaustible supply of experience that stood for everything life at my parent's house did not.
>
> (Williams, 2010, p. 16)

*****

> My mother had a sixth sense for when we were off-guard or feeling a bit calmer or had got some enjoyment elsewhere, away from her and the house. It was these moments that triggered the explosions of violence. . . . By the time I was four, I knew never to make any further demands on her and, wherever possible, to make myself invisible.
>
> (Williams, 2022, p. 23)

*****

> Sometimes, remembering that pain takes my breath away. It used to sneak up on me, catching me unaware, and double me over. I would break into a cold sweat, feel as though I should open my veins and bleed out whatever toxin was causing so much pain, even if that would mean death. Because death would feel better than this. Still today, every now and then – maybe once a year – I will physically remember that pain, and I weep for that younger self who walked around the world, excelled at school, sang in my church choir, tried to make friends, or fall in love or just grow up, while carrying this pain.
>
> (Klott et al., 2025, p. 4)

*****

> Other sessions, I didn't know what to say. I would sit there staring at you, wanting to explain what was happening inside of me but not having the words to tell you. I wished (and sometimes still do) that you could do a Vulcan mind meld

because finding the words, creating a language where you could see the world I lived in, felt impossible. . . . Do you remember those sessions when I couldn't find words? It seems impossible to believe now, because I can fill hours full and still have more to say.

(Klott et al., 2025, p. 8)

*****

The most painful category I've found myself in once I've revealed my trauma history is that of "damaged beyond repair."

(Klott et al., 2025, p. 10)

*****

But, when I met you, parts of me were also certain I was beyond repair. That it was just a matter of time before you, too, would know that I was a shattered person. That I was broken. And, worse, that I was despicable and needed to be avoided at all costs.

(Klott et al., 2025, p. 13)

*****

In that session, I expressed yet again how terrible it feels to love you so much and to know that I'm not as important to you as you are to me. I used the words "unrequited love" *for the first time* – it became so clear that it feels like just that – *a love that goes unmet.* And, I realized that it's how I felt throughout my child-hood, that I loved and loved and loved, and at best, I was tolerated, occasionally acknowledged, *but usually when something was taken from me.*

(Klott et al., 2025, p. 6)

Given the absence of maternal and paternal care (Craig, 2008; Crastnopol, 2015; Eaton, 2005), whether physically or mentally, the children described by Williams and Klott learn from early on how to "file away the ways that I can become needy and empty and bruised as evidence of my brokenness" (Klott et al., 2025, p. 11), finding love and trust ensnaring as it serves as a painful and traumatic prelude to further objectification, mischaracterization, and mis-"use" of self and body. Spon-taneous bodily expression of feeling alive suffers similar difficulties: all hunger unwanted and waning, body dissociation limed with body revulsion, and blank minds mingled, paradoxically, with a heightened sense of all surroundings;

I also could barely eat. I could go for days without eating much of anything.

(Klott et al., 2025, p. 12)

When I met you, I wasn't sure people remembered me after they were no longer with me. I was nearly certain that I disappeared for most people when I left the room. I was certain that if they did remember me, they didn't like me anymore. When I met you, I was certain that I constantly smelled bad.

(Klott et al., 2025, p. 12)

all in the service of the anti-life drive:

When I met you, I was certain that I would be dead before I made it to 40. In fact, I was somewhat surprised to have made it all the way to 28. I would hear voices talking about my death. One would say, *"What happened to her?"* The response *would* be, *"She killed herself." Just those two sentences. Nothing else.*

(Klott et al., 2025, p. 13; italics added)

What happened to her
She killed herself
Just two sentences
Nothing else

Two sentences that reveal a dark ontology of *innocence lost* (Kalsched, 2013) – a true hauntology signifying intergenerational lack and anti-life injunctions seemingly impossible to escape. Klott's and William's writing hauntingly reminds us that the very injunctions the Gone Child is born into further tragic ensnarement in the form of Fairbairn's desirable deserters (Cooper, 2000; Eigen, 1999, 2001; Shengold, 1999, 2011). That is, needed relationships promising safety, connection, even spiritual resurrection and renewal prove un"Faith"ful, furthering self-alienation;

Yet, despite it saving my life, attaching to him [stepfather] also meant that he was able to leave lasting damage that is hard to repair. Because I attached more to him than anyone else, he had so much more say over the development of my personhood than either of my biological parents. *His is the voice I hear most often, the one that integrated into my own voice, so that his judgments and comparisons live in me. His inconsistent message of my worth is the source of my inconsistent sense of self.*

(Klott et al., 2025, p. 21)

That teacher took this need and sexualized it.

(Klott et al., 2025, p. 32)

That interview with the Prosecuting Attorney (PA) was traumatizing. . . . She wanted to know if I worked with abused children. I'd said that I did. She suddenly switched gears and asked why I hadn't reported the abuse by Bob and my stepfathers earlier. . . . The PA then sat back and asked me how I could live with myself.

(Klott et al., 2025, p. 48)

> Being a member of that church likely saved my life. . . . This greatly sheltered me from most of what my peers were doing, and it gave me a chance to psychologically detox from the hyper-sexualization of my earlier life. I gained a community of people looking out for me. . . . Unfortunately, after awhile, that church became a shame-inducing place for me.
>
> (Klott et al., 2025, p. 62)

Symbolically, Dr. Klott's sensitive writing also brings to life a lived catastrophe I refer to as enforced *soul/ego-nudity*. The Gone Child frequently functions as the sole object of the desirous, predatory, and narcissistic "vision" of the Other. Not only are our Gone Children the recipients of the *confusion of tongues* throughout their painful histories, but they remain subject, continuously so, to the most profound forms of shaming of the self through the erosion of their privacy and dignity (by loved ones and trusted others). Trusted others include invited adults in the home context as well as our social-cultural institutions, which would include the church, the judicial system (judicial betrayal), and psychiatric-psychological milieus (Milner, 1981, 1988, 1994). Mileus frighteningly unaware of their own desirous gaze, their own stripping and imprisoning capacities, shaming the Gone Child into further hiddenness and self-loathing spirals, lacking in true authority – the authority of tenderness.

William's Authority of Tenderness and the Importance of Ontological Psychoanalysis

> And, from the beginning you've listened to the parts of me that long to heal, to connect to others, to have mutual relationships with others. From the beginning, I could feel that you saw the child in me longing to be understood and heard and cared about. *It was one of the most relieving and terrifying things back then, because I feared it would disappear without warning.* That's what I remember most about the beginning – knowing that someone was willing to be right there with me for the long haul and the fear that it was a dream, an illusion that would disappear.
>
> (Klott et al., 2025, p. 14; italics added)

Poignantly described by Dr. Klott, the presence of genuine connection revivifies healing longing in the midst of damage (Eigen, 2004). Finding *Objects of Hope* (Cooper, 2000) nourishes the ontological self's potential for a new beginning – although terrifying. It is also evident in Dr. Klott's writing that such revivification calls forth a holding able to, in the enduring words of Wordsworth (2004), survive the shadowy recollections of our first affections to find a *Faith* "that looks through death" (Wordsworth, 2004, p. 163). What kind of psychoanalysis is called forth, and what type of language is needed to meet such soul revealment?

Psychoanalysis as a vocation has long been influenced by two strands of healing. For Ogden (2019, 2022), the two strands can be defined as *epistemological psychoanalysis* and the other, *ontological psychoanalysis*. For Williams (2022), the two strands can be described as the psychoanalysis of the *Developmental Self* and the other, the psychoanalysis of the *Real Self.* Most schools and theorists of psychoanalysis may have a preference or allegiance to one of the strands of thought. For Ogden (2019), epistemological psychoanalysis focuses on arriving at an understanding of unconscious meaning, whereas,

> From the perspective of ontological psychoanalysis, it is not the knowledge arrived at by the patient and analyst that is the central point; rather, it is the patient's experience of "arriving at understanding creatively and with immense joy," an experience in which the patient is engaged not predominantly in search of self-understanding, but in *experiencing* the process of becoming more fully himself.
>
> (Ogden, 2022, p. 13)

Williams further mentions that; "Successful analysis, in my opinion, draws a distinction between the Developmental Self of the individual, in need of *assistance*, and the True Self, in need of solitude and dignity" (2022, p. xiv). Hayuta Gurevich (2016) would also add to the latter two strands as the theory and practice of Oedipal psychoanalysis as compared to Orphic psychoanalysis, that is, the psychoanalysis of Ferenczi, Winnicott, Eigen, Ogden, and many others (Orphic), in relation to Freud and ego psychology (Oedipal). Orphic analysis, or the analysis of the *unlived life* (Ogden, 2005), provides a profound understanding and holding of those analysands exposed to lack, callousness, profound objectification, predation, confusion of tongues, and more. An approach that aims to enliven the analysand by turning traumatic flashbacks into hauntings, as articulated by Klott, re-inviting Gone children to relating and hope;

> I call it a *haunting* and not a flashback because I no longer experience the all-encompassing take-over of my mind that happened when I had active flashbacks. Instead, it now feels like the ghosts of the past remind me of their existence, but I am not lost in the scenes from which they were born. . . . It bothers me that I needed your assurance. Yet, it is also a reminder to myself that to be attached to another is to allow them to help when I'm distressed and not a sign of being needy or wanting too much.
>
> (Klott et al, 2025, p. 20)

From Dr. Raubolt, the Orphic attitude is expressed as follows:

> As is summarized in Emmi Pikler's work (2019), the relationship is all. It is a matter of life for the child.
>
> (Klott et al., 2025, p. 16)

I was fortunate that one of my first supervisors in graduate school taught me to go beyond the clinical hour in providing therapy. *The well-being, sometimes the very lives of people we see, can hang by a single thread. I learned to extend myself, thoughtfully but with determination.* My supervisor closed his every letter to me for over 30 years with *"In the Struggle Together."*

(Klott et al., 2025, p. 50)

Being in the struggle together reads very similar to Leston Haven's *A Safe Space* (1989), finding Dr. Raubolt remaining a firm and gentle presence, allowing, in Emmi Pikler's psychoanalytic approach, Dr. Klott's resilient capacities ("I feel as though my resilient self shows up in the therapy office"; Klott et al., 2025, p. 87), her natural impetus towards connection and ego-expansion to slowly unfold, gently facilitating her natural engagement and need for self-discovery in connection to another. Holding, facilitation, and later moments of "play" remained central as compared to Dr. Klott's earlier exposure to pedagogical approaches (CBT, etc.). Respecting the expression of emotion as needed and legitimate, rather than offering distractions as found in current technique-focused therapies, is also of importance to Dr. Raubolt and the Orphic-ontological psychoanalyst. A true welcoming presence, actively observing and fully present, available, responsive, and receptive in the face of ontological terror (Laing, 1960). Here Dr. Raubolt not only links with the work of Ferenczi when he wrote on the need for a different outcome for traumatized souls but actually furthers the psychoanalytic holding, similar to the work of Ofra Eshel (2005, 2010, 2013, 2019) and her treatment of an incarcerated analysand (also in Bloch & Daws, 2015), or Michael Eigen's response to a suicidal analysand in stating "I will jump with you" (Eigen, 2001, p. 58), effectively enlarging the psychoanalytic field, ensuring the provision of primary experience outside[2] the consulting room in a courageous way:

> Theoretically, my stance originates in how I define a New, Real, Transformative therapeutic relationship as extending beyond the four protective walls composing office space. I have come to believe a therapist/analyst can only offer safety and protectiveness if there is sufficient courage to take considered risks on the patient's behalf. Therapists should be prepared to use their clinical standing and resources on behalf of their complex trauma patients. Since words have served to structure a language of betrayal dramatic, courageous, and honest action where the therapist is tested in real-time and place may be required.
>
> (Klott et al., 2025, p. 51)

The bottom line is that the therapist must continuously attempt to respond to the patient's needs in a way that:

1) Feels alive, real, and beneficial for both of them.
2) Creates and reinforces a sense of we-ness between them.
3) Transfers his sense of power, strength, and knowledge to the patient as naturally and smoothly as possible.
4) Allows the patient to empower and acknowledge herself for her own achievements (by remaining as much as possible humbly behind but firmly supportive of the patient's progressions).

(Klott et al., 2025, pp. 26–27)

Both analyst and analysand move between two worlds, an unfolding mutuality even if asymmetrical, ensuring a psychic buoyancy able to navigate the storms of life:

> Luckily, I'd settled enough into the attachment that I could count on you for the things that came next. I didn't realize that my childhood trauma was about to interrupt my adult life in a much more tangible way than through processing memories in therapy, but that is exactly what happened in our sixth year of treatment. Everything would become so chaotic and terrifying, but I'd established enough attachment that I was able to lean into my relationship with you. This is what buoyed me as the waves threatened to capsize me.
>
> (Klott et al., 2025, p. 36)

> So, Raubolt, here we are some 20 years later. Through the "we" of our therapy relationship, I have been able to reclaim so many parts of myself that were terribly wounded by severe, complex childhood trauma that reverberated into my adulthood. It took both of us and the co-created "we" to get me here. I'm grateful to both of us for our willingness to do this work, and I'm curious about where we will find ourselves as we move into this new phase of treatment.
>
> (Klott et al., 2025, p. 100)

Re-Visioning Childe Harold's Pilgrimage and Dr. Klott's "Hope"

As I reluctantly take leave of the writing relationship created by Drs Klott and Raubolt, infused with their mutual capacity for tenderness and sustaining psychoanalytic love, I am filled with deep affection and gratitude. A Faith in the self and other reborn and a faith in growth and connection restored. In this, I end with Dr. Klott's psychoanalytic hope as well as with Lord Byron George Gordon's writing on the *Children of the Second Birth*;

> As you read this book, we hope that you will witness the possibility of healing profound trauma. In a field that sometimes portrays a kind of hopelessness disguised in clinical labels, we tell the story of how together (patient and analyst) can create a relational foundation from which healing could take hold. In the telling of this story, we hope you will notice the characteristics we each bring to this healing relationship and that your observations will lead to a deepening of your understanding of trauma and the psychotherapy that can mend those damaged by it.
>
> (Klott et al., 2025, p. xiii)

With this in mind, we may find, again, Lord Byron's *Children of the Second Birth* (1812/2006), the cosmic nomads that serve through their experience as our dream weavers, constantly defying gravity, soaring beyond boundaries, reminding us all that the psychic universe is creatively wild and infinitely mysterious.

Notes

1　I recalled a childhood book that served as a symbol of my own psychological survival, *The Survivors* [*Die Oorlewendes*] (1984) by Johan Bredell.
2　Also see Dr. Raubolt's use of transitional objects: "Toward the end of the session we had just before I was to go to the interview, you handed me this small clay car. It had been on your bookcase for years, and I'd wondered about it. I'd imagined a young patient had made it for you. I'd actually wished I could have made something for you to keep near by. Raubolt, you told me that the car had been made by your son when he was a child, and you wanted me to take it with me to the interview. You told me to remember your office while I was there, to remember that you were going to be in your quiet, peace-filled office when I got back. I hesitated, shocked by the offer, but you insisted. This act of kindness was one of the most powerful moments in my attaching to you. The fact that you would allow me to not only touch something so valuable as your child's creation but to insist I take it with me to a place so frightening told me that you understood that I would need to know you were with me in some way" (Klott et al., 2025, p. 72).

Bibliography

Bion, W. R. (1990). *A Memoir of the Future*. Routledge.

Blanton, S. (1971). *Diary of My Analysis with Sigmund Freud*. Hawthorn Books, Inc.

Bloch, S., and Daws, L. (2015). *Living Moments: On the Work of Michael Eigen*. Karnac Books.

Bollas, B. (2013). *Catch Them before They Fall: The Psychoanalysis of Breakdown*. Routledge.

Borgogno, F. (2021). *One Life Heals Another: Beginnings, Maturity, Outcomes of a Vocation*. IP Books.

Brandchaft, B., Doctors, S., and Sorter. D. (2010). *Towards an Emancipatory Psychoanalysis: Brandchaft's Intersubjective Vision*. Routledge.

Bredell, J. (1984). *The Survivors* [*Die Oorlewendes*]. Daan Retief Uitgewers.

Burnett, F. H. (1905/2024). *A Little Princess*. Charles Scribner's Sons.

Byron, G. G. (1812/2006). *Selected Poems of Lord George Gordon Byron*. In S. J. Wolfson, & J. O. Hayden (Ed.). Penguin Classics.

Cooper, S. H. (2000). *Object of Hope-Exploring Possibility and Limit in Psychoanalysis*. The Analytic Press.

Craig, E. (2008). The human and the hidden existential wondering about depth, soul, and the unconscious. *Humanistic Psychologist*, *36*, 227–282.

Crastnopol, M. (2015). *Micro-Trauma: A Psychoanalytic Understanding of Cumulative Psychic Injury*. Routledge.

Eastman, G. (2014). *Freeing the Imprisoned Self: A Memoir*. Dog Ear Publishing.

Eaton, J. E. (2005). The obstructive object. *Psychoanalytic Review*, *92*(3), 355–372.

Eigen, M. (1977). On working with "unwanted" patients. *International Journal of Psychoanalysis*, *58*, 109–121.

Eigen, M. (1981). The area of faith in Winnicott, Lacan, and Bion. *International Journal of Psychoanalysis*, *62*, 413–433.

Eigen, M. (1983). Dual union or undifferentiation? A critique of Marion Milner's view of the sense of psychic creativeness. *International Review of Psychoanalysis*, *10*, 415–428.

Eigen, M. (1985). Toward Bion's starting point: Between catastrophe and faith. *International Journal of Psychoanalysis*, *66*, 321–330.

Eigen, M. (1986). *The Psychotic Core*. Karnac, 2004.

Eigen, M. (1992). *Coming through the Whirlwind*. Chiron Publications.

Eigen, M. (1993). *The Electrified Tightrope*. Edited by A. Phillips. Karnac, 2004.

Eigen, M. (1995). Psychic deadness: Freud. *Contemporary. Journal of Psychoanalysis, 31,* 277–299.

Eigen, M. (1996). *Psychic Deadness.* Karnac, 2004.

Eigen, M. (1999). *Toxic Nourishment.* Karnac.

Eigen, M. (2001). *Damaged Bonds.* Karnac.

Eigen, M. (2004). *The Sensitive Self.* Wesleyan University Press.

Eigen, M. (2007). *Feeling Matters.* Karnac.

Eigen, M. (2008). Healing longing in the midst of damage. *Psychoanalytic Dialogues, 15*(2), 169–183.

Eigen, M. (2009). *Flames from the Unconscious: Trauma, Madness and Faith.* Karnac.

Eigen, M. (2010). *Eigen in Seoul vol 1: Madness and Murder.* Karnac.

Eigen, M. (2011a). *Eigen in Seoul vol 2: Faith and Transformation.* Karnac.

Eigen, M. (2011b). *Contact with the Depths.* Karnac.

Eigen, M. (2012). *Kabbalah and Psychoanalysis.* Karnac.

Eigen, M. (2018). *The Challenge of Being Human.* Routledge.

Eigen, M., and Daws, L. (2019). *Dialogues with Eigen: Psyche Singing.* Routledge.

Elkin, H. (1972). On selfhood and the development of ego structures in infancy. *The Psychoanalytic Review, 59,* 389–416.

Eshel, O. (2005). Pentheus rather than Oedipus: On perversion, survival and analytic "presencing." *International Journal of Psychoanalysis, 86,* 1071–1097.

Eshel, O. (2010). Patient – analyst interconnectedness: Personal notes on close encounters of a new dimension. *Psychoanalytic. Inquiry, 30,* 146–154.

Eshel, O. (2013). Patient-analyst "witness": On analytic "presencing," passion, and compassion in states of breakdown, despair, and deadness. *Psychoanalytic. Quarterly, 82,* 925–963.

Eshel, O. (2019). *The Emergence of Analytic Oneness: Into the Heart of Psychoanalysis.* Routledge.

Gordon, B. G. (1812). *Childe Harold's Pilgrimage.* Edited by G. Hernandez. Independent Publishing Platform.

Grotstein, J. S. (1997). Integrating one-person and two-person psychologies: Autochthony and alterity in counterpoint. *Psychoanalytic Quarterly, 66,* 403–430.

Guntrip, H. (1975). My experience of analysis with Fairbairn and Winnicott: How complete a result does psycho-analytic therapy achieve? *International Review of Psychoanalysis, 2,* 145–156.

Gurevich, H. (2016). Orpha, Orphic functions, and the Orphic analyst: Winnicott's "regression to dependence" in the language of Ferenczi. *The American Journal of Psychoanalysis, 76,* 322–340.

Havens, L. (1989). *A Safe Space: Laying the Groundwork of Psychotherapy.* Harvard University Press.

Kalsched, D. (2013). *Trauma and the Soul – a Psycho-Spiritual Approach to Human Development and Its Interruption.* Routledge.

Khan, M. R. (1963). The concept of cumulative trauma. *Psychoanalytic Study of the Child, 18,* 286–306.

Laing, R. D. (1960). *The Divided Self.* Tavistock.

Marcus, P. (1999). *Autonomy in the Extreme Situation: Bruno Bettelheim, the Nazi Concentration Camps and the Mass Society.* Praeger Publications.

Milner, A. (1981). *Thou Shalt Not Be Aware: Society's Betrayal of the Child.* A Meridian Book.

Milner, A. (1988). *Banished Knowledge: Facing Childhood Injuries.* Doubleday.

Milner, A. (1994). *For Your Own Good: Hidden Cruelty in Child Rearing and the Roots of Violence.* Noonday Press.

Moser, T. (1977). *Years of Apprenticeship on the Couch: Fragments of My Training Analysis.* Urizen Books.

Ogden, T. H. (2005). *This Art of Psychoanalysis-Dreaming, Undreamt Dreams and Interrupted Cries*. Routledge.

Ogden, T. H. (2019). Ontological psychoanalysis or "what do you want to be when you grow up?" *The Psychoanalytic Quarterly*, *88*(4), 661–684.

Ogden, T. H. (2022). *Coming to Life in the Consulting Room*. Routledge.

Parens, H. (2004). *Renewal of Life: Healing from the Holocaust*. Schreiber Publishing.

Pikler, E. (2019). *The Pikler Approach: A Parenting Guide*. Translated by P. W. L. Murray. Routledge.

Reichbart, R. (2022). *Anatomy of a Psychotic Experience*. IP Books.

Rogers, A. G. (1995). *A Shining Affliction*. Penguin Viking.

Rogers, A. G. (2006). *The Unsayable: The Hidden Language of Trauma*. Random House.

Rogers, A. G. (2016). *Incandescent Alphabets: Psychosis and the Enigma of Language*. Karnac, Routledge, 2018.

Rothenberg, R. E. (2001). *The Jewel in the Wound: How the Body Expresses the Needs of the Psyche and Offers a Path to Transformation*. Chiron Publications.

Sawyer, A. P. (2015). *Smoking, Cigarettes, Eating Glass: A Psychologist's Memoir*. SFWP Publications.

Shengold, L. (1999). *Soul Murder: Thoughts about Therapy, Hate, Love, and Memory*. Yale University Press.

Shengold, L. (2011). Trauma, soul murder, and change. *Psychoanalytic Quarterly*, *80*(1), 121–138.

Summers, F. (2005). *Self-Creation: Psychoanalytic Therapy and the Art of the Possible*. The Analytic Press.

Von Drigalski, D. (1979). *Flowers on Granite: One Woman's Odyssey through Psychoanalysis*. Creative Arts Book Company.

Williams, P. (2010). *The Fifth Element*. Karnac Books.

Williams, P. (2013). *Scum*. Karnac Books.

Williams, P. (2022). *The Authority of Tenderness: Dignity and the True Self in Psychoanalysis*. Karnac Books.

Winnicott, D. W. (1958). The capacity to be alone. *International Journal of Psychoanalysis*, *39*, 416–420.

Winnicott, D. W. (1969). The use of an object. *International Journal of Psychoanalysis*, *50*, 711–716.

Wordsworth, W. (2004). *Selected Poems*. Penguin Classics.

Young-Bruehl, E. (2012). *Childism: Confronting Prejudice against Children*. Yale University Press.

Index

For Product Safety Concerns and Information please contact our EU
representative GPSR@taylorandfrancis.com
Taylor & Francis Verlag GmbH, Kaufingerstraße 24, 80331 München, Germany

9 7 8 1 0 3 2 9 9 5 3 8 0